ATHLETE FOR LIFE

PUBLISHING, LLC

ATHLETE
—FOR—
LIFE

OMARI FAULKNER

Athlete for Life

Copyright ©2019 Omari Faulkner

All rights reserved. No part of this book may be reproduced or transmitted in any form or by any means without permission in writing from the author.

The author has made every effort to ensure the accuracy of the information within this book was correct at time of publication. The author does not assume and hereby disclaims any liability to any party for any loss, damage, or disruption caused by errors or omissions, whether such errors or omissions result from accident, negligence, or any other cause.

ISBN-13: 978-1-7339610-7-3
ISBN-10: 1-7339610-7-0
(Paperback Edition)

ISBN-13: 978-1-7339610-3-5
ISBN-10-1-7339610-3-5
(eBook Edition)

Library of Congress Control Number: 2019904236

Published by West 27th Publishing, LLC

Cover Design by Brilliant Creative Studio

Author Photo by Rafael Suanes

Interior Typesetting and Layout by Melissa Williams Design

*Dedicated in memory of Michael D. Moody
(January 15, 1981–March 10, 2000)*

My "Forever" Teammate; a true example of an Athlete for Life

May you forever rest in paradise . . .

CONTENTS

Preface ix

Introduction xi

Chapter 1—*Transforming Insanity* 1

Chapter 2—*Expand Your View* 13

Chapter 3—*Managing Time* 24

Chapter 4—*Take Control of Your Message* 35

Chapter 5—*Find Your Music* 50

Chapter 6—*Coaches Blaze the Trail* 64

Chapter 7—*The College Cafeteria* 75

Chapter 8—*Transcending Struggles* 88

Chapter 9—*Parents, Thank You* 98

Conclusion 108

Acknowledgments 121

About the Author 127

PREFACE

As an active member of the Navy Reserve, one component of my Reserve commitments is two weeks of annual training (AT). In 2017, I conducted my AT in Newport, Rhode Island, at the United States Naval War College. Before departing on this trip, I committed to writing the basic foundations of this book. I knew that I'd have no commitments after work and on the weekends. Once I took off my uniform, I wrote for hours, late into the night, and repeated this process over and over. I'd take a break to absorb the Newport American history, and then I'd write and write and write. I even did something I never do as much as I think I should: I took in the sunset one memorable evening. It was lovely, and a moment I will never forget. It was in Newport that I set out to accomplish a mission, and among these pages are the results of countless hours of reflection, interviews and a road map for you to make a positive commitment wherever you are in your jouney.

Today I wear many hats. When someone asks, "What do you do?" or "What line of work are you in?" I oftentimes stumble through the response. Why? Because I don't just do one thing. I work within the federal government solutions arena, and I also teach graduate courses on international diplomacy, sports leadership and management, global games, etc. I advise governors and local government officials on issues that range from education and housing to economic development and volunteering. I'm a dedicated youth coach and active Navy public affairs officer. I speak to audiences across the country and around the world, and I am an author.

I am an athlete!

Through my student-athlete experience, I taught myself how to effectively manage multiple competing priorities, set time-management schedules, improve my communication skills, drive toward my goals and much more. I encourage you to document your journey through the *Athlete for Life* manual. Whatever method you choose, I promise you will thank yourself later, and all the student-athletes that you share your story with will also thank you.

Enjoy the book, and create your journey.

INTRODUCTION

An Athlete for Life

If you are reading this, you probably belong to one of five groups: you're a current or previous student-athlete, a coach and/or administrator tasked with leading and managing student-athletes, a parent of a student-athlete, a supporter of student athletics or maybe a novice—you picked up a sport or athletic activity and you are interested in applying the skills you are learning to work positively for you—for life! Maybe, like me, you're a bit of all the above.

This manual is written in such a way that you can read, study and absorb the information at your own pace. If you want to start at the final chapter and read backward, the book will produce the same results as if you start from the beginning and read in chronological order. Feel free to jump around and explore. This is your journey. In these pages, you'll learn the techniques and approaches to becoming an **Athlete for Life**.

PAY IT FORWARD

I wrote this book to highlight the importance of connecting with the athlete in all of us—to further define the lessons learned through our athletic experiences: if you played one year of varsity track and field in high school, or you were on the rowing-club team in college or you've become a cyclist or an avid runner or the starting fullback at a major Division I program, you are an athlete!

WHAT IS AN ATHLETE FOR LIFE?

As I mentioned before, our journeys will all be different: just as each artist begins with a different canvas, a different set of tools and a different approach, so will each athlete have different outcomes—some may never again play the sport they once loved (or didn't really love) once the competitive period of their lives ends. Some may continue playing the sport they love well into their sixties and beyond. Regardless of your path, being an **Athlete for Life** has nothing to do with how long you play a particular sport, nor how long you remain physically active. It has everything to do with balancing multiple priorities as a student-athlete, understanding the importance of your academic studies and the ability to be the best student-athlete and teammate that you are capable of becoming.

You become an Athlete for Life when you positively apply the academic and educational lessons you've learned in the classroom and the life skills you've learned through sports to your everyday life.

Doing so allows you to become more prepared to climb the mountains of life, see through those cloudy days and maintain your focus through peak success periods—you are continuously learning and teaching others how to combine academic and athletic excellence. While your days as a competitive athlete will someday end, you can still approach each day, obstacle and success as you would on the field, track, court, pool or wherever.

My student-athlete journey officially began in the eighth grade and brought me to Georgetown University on a full scholarship to play basketball for the school of my dreams. Before arriving on the Hilltop in Washington, DC, I could have benefited from a book like *Athlete for Life*. This is a manual which will guide student-athletes to maximize the athletic and academic experiences they encounter; it will hone and harness their skills and successfully propel them throughout life's journey—the game will never stop if you become an **Athlete for Life**, but first you must learn how.

Early in my collegiate athletic career, I let sports define me; I had blinders on. It was a disastrous pattern, and it's a really easy one for many student-athletes to fall into. But that was only one side of my experience; the other side recognized and utilized the balance, focus and determination that helped me become a successful student-athlete. Once I removed the blinders, everything I learned in the classroom and on the court morphed me into the successful son, business leader, father, international diplomat, speaker, mentor and author I always knew I could become.

THE ATHLETE FOR LIFE MANUAL

In this book you'll learn how the student-athlete experience is a lifelong journey that you create. The very principles learned through my student-athlete experience led me directly to opportunities beyond my imagination, in particular being selected as a US Department of State cultural envoy. I represented the United States government in more than forty-five countries, using sports as the engine to power understanding, trust and relationship-building with many people who had never engaged directly with Americans before. To this very day, I consider that one of the most amazing professional experiences I've ever had, and had it not been for my days as a student-athlete, I know I could not have shown the leadership that was required in many situations.

Throughout this book, I use my personal stories to navigate and highlight the importance of the techniques and approaches you'll need to discover and uncover that will sharpen the **Athlete for Life** within you.

In Chapter 1, you'll delve into the immersive

nature of the student-athlete's experience and the transitions that take place when you move to that next level. When juggling athletics and academics, life can easily become overwhelming. Add the inevitable disappointments every athlete faces into the mix, and you're completely in over your head. Taking the lead and finding balance is the key to staying in the game.

Chapter 2 will be all about how to see both the trees and the forest. Sometimes people miss the bigger picture as they focus on situations in those moments. The big picture and the details are both important. You'll learn how to expand the view of your current situation. As a student-athlete you are in a resource-rich environment, and we will walk through specific steps to achieve benefits from these resources. Finally, I'll explain how you can fly like an eagle by tapping into your limitless potential.

In Chapter 3, I illustrate how important time management is to balance the rigors of being a student-athlete. As athletes, we can go all day, but it is easy to get behind and lose focus. I will discuss the benefits of having the opportunity to develop your own time-management principles early, and how to develop a system to put those principles to work for yourself throughout life. The sooner you master time management, the better!

In Chapter 4, I demonstrate how building your network is paramount to your future success. Much of it will not happen immediately, but I will explain how building relationships is an incredibly powerful instrument toward your development. You'll discover and understand how you are fully in control of your brand, and I will share actions that you can take today that show results immediately and others that will plant seeds that will grow later in your career.

I love music, and Chapter 5 is all about that. You may or may not be a music connoisseur, yet in this chapter you will learn how to find your signature tune, create your own music and take full control of your academic future. We will again discuss the importance of capitalizing on the resources afforded you and stepping outside of your comfort zone. Most notably, you will understand the importance of selecting areas of study that not only interest you but motivate you as well.

Chapter 6 is dedicated to coaches and the unique role they play in developing tomorrow's leaders, today's student-athletes and **Athletes for Life**. I explain just how important the coaching profession is. As a player, I never fully understood the role of a coach; I never saw the behind-the-scenes work and preparation that coaches undertake, but now I understand. To the coaches out there: your role is vital. Your physical and mental health are as important to the success of your players as anything else, and in this chapter, I offer you some advice to benefit you not only as a coach but as a person.

In Chapter 7, we will further explore the options available to you on a college campus. The college campus isn't the forest: life is the forest, and this book will help you prepare for that. Nevertheless, on campus there are many trees that can be used for different purposes and utilized at different stages in your life.

Chapter 8 is focused on mental transcendence. We can never get too far removed from the importance of the little things that matter most in our lives. Being a student-athlete isn't always easy: much is expected of you by others, and you expect a lot from yourself. In this chapter, I provide simple tips for finding time to unwind and enjoy where you are in life, even if only for a short period. These tips will rejuvenate your mental wellness, which will allow you to be at your very best.

Finally, if you are a parent, guardian or mentor to a student-athlete, Chapter 9 is just for you.

MY WRITING JOURNEY

I cannot count the number of times I attempted to write something that would help other student-athletes avoid the pitfalls I experienced throughout high school and college. I'd begin to write, and then I'd change the direction of the book. Then one day, I simply asked myself, *What type of book would have helped you, your teammates and fellow student-athletes?* At that moment, this book's concept was full steam ahead. I had countless conversations with parents, coaches, players and sport leaders around the globe, and I was motivated by their stories.

In these pages I pull back the curtain and share many stories that I've never spoken about to a large public audience. Some events are very personal, but I felt it was important to share these moments, as many student-athletes encounter similar situations on a daily basis, and I wanted to provide a manual that would provide effective guidance.

I also want parents, administrators, mentors, colleges and universities and other organizations who support our student-athletes to use *Athlete for Life* as one instrument that helps propel young minds to think outside the box of their current circumstances and believe there is more to life and more to themselves than the sport they play.

I eventually decided that being a basketball player would no longer define who I was, and in doing so, I applied the same drive I had for sports to multiple areas of my life.

It's easy for a young athlete to let life get out of balance, but at the same time, a college or university setting is the perfect place to attain that balance. In *Athlete for Life*, I provide real-life examples and methods for student-athletes to achieve the greatness they desire in sports yet the balance required to succeed throughout life.

The life of a student-athlete is full of pitfalls and traps, but it can also provide you with structure, rewards and goals—everything you need to be a success in whatever you end up doing. You just need to know what the traps are—and what appropriate tools will guide you through your journey.

I could not be more grateful that I chose to be an athlete. I thank God for giving me the ability to play a sport I enjoyed, learned from and continue to find amazement in even today.

Don't keep your **Athlete for Life** story to yourself—share it. You can connect with all your fellow athletes on social media using #AthleteForLife on Twitter and Instagram.

CHAPTER 1

Transforming Insanity

That's insane! This was and still is the usual response I receive from people who are not familiar with the workload and responsibilities of being a student-athlete. Then I let people into the everyday grind and the hours of practice that no one sees, and with amazement, the questions continue. *You practiced how long? You played basketball by yourself in the rain? When did you have time for studying? When did you have time to do anything else?* Oftentimes these conversations conclude with the person saying, *You are insane!*

Maybe you're a previous or current student-athlete, a coach and/or administrator tasked with leading and managing student-athletes, the parent of a student-athlete or a supporter of student athletics.

If you are like me, you're all the above! No matter which group(s) you're in, you are probably insane, my friend.

What other word would you use? You're voluntarily signing up for the student-athlete life, an arduous journey that can't be strategized or won alone. You have to embrace and navigate this insanity because the road will continuously challenge you along the way.

Once you transition from one phase of your student-athlete journey to the next, everything as you know it changes—holidays, time with family and friends, summer breaks, competition, everything. For example, my transition from middle school to high school was intense—the practice schedule and the approach to the game intensified. In middle school, we focused more on skill-building and understanding the importance of each person's role on the team; in high school, time and emphasis were placed on strength and conditioning, to keep up with the faster, stronger competition.

Next came college, and that was an even bigger change. I'm six-feet-six, and for half of my high-school career, I was the tallest person on my team, or sometimes second by one inch. In college, six players were taller than me. I vividly remember the first practice I went up against my seven-feet-tall teammate Ruben Boumtje Boumtje: I hit the deck hard. But I always got back up and challenged him again. He was and still is a gentle giant and one of the nicest people you'll ever meet. I had to make rapid adjustments to how I played because college was a completely new level.

Each phase of transition looks and feels different. You may have felt like your life was different from most people's before, but the insanity will only intensify. You may not believe that—you've been playing your particular sport for years, and you've been a student since kindergarten—so what could be so different in college? Well, everything!

MAJOR TRANSITION

Right after my high-school graduation, I arrived at Georgetown's historic campus, overlooking the Potomac River in Washington, DC, to begin a five-week academic program called the Community Scholars Program. The program was established to provide multicultural students from first-generation college families the opportunity to study, attend workshops and, most importantly, form bonds with fellow students and faculty members. It would be a turning point in life—my first activity as a college student!

I walked through the front gates to be met by a familiar face: Mike Riley, an assistant coach in men's basketball. He warmly greeted me, my mom and stepdad. I had met Coach Riley in person on my official visit to Georgetown months before, when he told me his personal story. He had grown up in the DC area playing basketball and later joined the Navy before playing for the Hoyas himself. He knew all about the program and had a firm fidelity to the Georgetown community. During the visit, he drove me all around DC—we talked and connected, and the way he welcomed me and my family was very impressive to a Southern boy like myself.

On that hot summer day, we exchanged chitchat as he led me to the dorm in which I'd live that summer. Then he casually mentioned that I needed to be down at the gym by six o' clock to play in a summer-league game. *A game!?* I thought. I expected a longer introduction to take in the fact that I was on a college campus as a student. I wanted to wander around campus with my mom and take in the moment.

Well, I had asked for this reality, I had envisioned it and it was here. I had wanted to be a top-level Division I student-athlete, and now I was.

I went down to the gym a couple hours later and put on a Pro City Kenner League uniform. My first game on the Georgetown campus! The Kenner League had (and still has) deep roots in the DC community, dating back to the early 1980s. The best of the best play in this league, and there I was, not even four hours into my college career. I was now in the game.

As I walked onto the floor, I thought, *This is unreal!*

You'd think I'd remember everything about the game, but I don't. The one thing I remember is the crowd. I looked around and saw so many Georgetown alumni in the stands, mostly members of the Hoya Hoop Club (HHC), a volunteer organization that supports the men's basketball program. This was their opportunity to see the incoming freshman class for the first time, and they showed up in hefty numbers.

There I was and, unbeknownst to me then, I would later come to appreciate the role of the HHC members, but not until years after graduating from Georgetown. Allow me to digress for a moment. Almost five to six years after I played my final game in a Hoya uniform, I sought to become more active in the club. I wanted to provide an active example to current and future student-athletes. I did just that: I would meet other members after work on weekdays to do fundraising cold calls on behalf of Georgetown basketball. I loved entering an empty arena early on Saturday mornings to put out thousands of T-shirts before the games, and I spent many late nights coordinating with volunteers, planning events, etc. This was grassroots volunteering with some of the most loyal and passionate Georgetown basketball fans. I did not hesitate for one second: Georgetown had built me, and it would be my honor to represent the HHC, so when I was nominated and elected to serve as the club's board secretary, it was a very proud moment for me, and one I will never forget.

Now back to the moment I walked onto the hardwood in a Hoya uniform . . .

The whole time I was in a daze—I just could not believe I was playing in a summer-league game in Washington, DC—but I do remember feeling gloomy whenever I looked into the crowd and saw my mother and stepdad: I longed to be alone with my mom to soak up our last moments before my college career started. But it wasn't to be. The next day, they'd travel back to their home in Georgia. Our final moments were special; I hugged my mother goodbye, and both of us were in tears as at all our leave-takings, even today. As I watched them drive away, it hit me: I'm in college, and I'm here alone.

That's when the insanity reached a new level. I was a Southern kid with a drawl so thick I needed subtitles—almost no one on campus that summer could understand me. It was hard to communicate with others in the Community Scholars Program, so I went back to the gym, the only place where I could pick up a ball, hone my craft and be understood. It was my comfort zone. But that turned out to be a mistake.

In December of my freshman year, just a few games into my Georgetown University career, our team was 9-0. We'd just beaten the University of Louisville on their home court, and my dad had driven from Memphis to Louisville, Kentucky, to see me play in college for the very first time.

After the game, I was livid. Why? Because I hadn't played a single minute in that game. I was fuming, disappointed that my father had watched as I sat on the bench the entire time. I felt as though I had let him down, as though I had made the wrong decision to attend Georgetown. Besides, why wouldn't Coach let me play a few minutes in front of my father? Was I really that bad of a player?

These thoughts were me succumbing to the insanity.

KNOW WHAT YOU'RE GETTING INTO

In order to handle the ups and downs of being a student-athlete, and navigate your new reality, you have to understand your new environment—especially what has changed.

Let me tell you a little secret about what you're about to step into.

College athletics (and athletics in general) are impossible to predict, so you have to maintain a balanced approach to your situation. To do that, look at the entire picture—not just what you don't have, but what you do have.

After the Louisville game, I was upset because of what I didn't have, and I allowed that to limit me. I felt I should have played more, but the reality was that I could neither predict nor control my coach's decisions; however, I could control my own behavior, and so can you.

TRANSFORMING INSANITY INTO ORGANIZED AND PRODUCTIVE SANITY

Oftentimes I am asked, *How did you turn things around?* This wasn't always the easiest question for me to answer. After some years, I was able to reflect and truly understand what drove me to positively transform myself during a period of frustration and what felt like total insanity. Now my answer to that question is simple: balance.

I achieved balance once I determined to do two things: challenge myself to work just as hard in the classroom as I did on the basketball court, and contribute to my team the best way I could. I listened to my heart.

Achieving balance isn't always the easiest task, but it isn't totally difficult. The foundation to balance is gaining control of the myriad priorities in your life. However, you can't allow a few to take control while others go abandoned.

After the Louisville game, I didn't have that balance. My entire sense of self relied on my basketball output. I neglected my academic priorities, so when things didn't go as I had planned on the basketball court, my equilibrium was disrupted. As a result, I isolated myself and became bitter in many ways. Just think: what type of teammate will you become if you are isolated and bitter?

To fully embrace the insanity of being a student-athlete, remember that you are implanted in a resource-rich environment, but a resource won't be effective unless you use it. (I discuss this more in Chapter 7, The College Cafeteria.) A car can't take you anywhere unless you get in and drive. Food can't provide nourishment for your body unless you eat it. And college won't improve your life unless you achieve academic and athletic balance and use what your university is offering you. This is the key to transforming insanity into organized and productive sanity, a primary ingredient to becoming an **Athlete for Life**.

I still had a scholarship to Georgetown, the university I had always dreamed of going to. I had accomplished a great deal through sports by never giving up. I figured, why not the same in the classroom? So I went for it. In my heart, being a stellar student-athlete was more important than anything else, so I sought to be more rounded, open-minded and connected to my environment. Doing so created a feeling of balance, which propelled me to new heights—I established new goals and found doors which had been there all along.

BECOMING A TEAM PLAYER

Once I achieved that balance in my student-athlete journey, I no longer felt isolated, and I let go of the bitter feelings. My focus pivoted toward my very own role on the team. I'd ask myself, *How can I make the team better? What can I do to be a better teammate?* In practice, I zoned in and pushed myself harder to motivate my teammates. In academics, I led by example and would call out anyone on the team not putting forth their best effort in the classroom. It wasn't in my comfort zone at first, but as a leader you know when you need to step out of comfort and get to work.

I'd actually enjoy pushing my teammates in practice, getting under their skin. My individual playing time decreased, but I evolved into a team player, which meant I would ensure my teammates were prepared. I sought to provide in practice the toughest competition they'd face, so during game time our team would be primed for success. And it worked.

A better teammate produces better results. You

will feel a sense of responsibility and a sense of pride when you contribute to the success of your team. In college, your role on the team may change significantly from what you had envisioned; taking responsibility and pride in your contributions to the team creates a sense of understanding of the mission and how you can make the greatest impact.

I will never forget watching Mike Sweetney, my freshman roommate, sitting at the circular tables at the NBA Draft, waiting to hear his name called. I was preparing for my senior year at Georgetown that summer, and I watched him live the dream: he was the number-eight pick and went to the New York Knicks. I couldn't have been happier for him and his family, knowing all the work I had seen him put into his craft. He made it! And I felt like it was I who had just been drafted: I was proud of the feeling that I'd helped him.

As a team you will fail together and you will win together, so ensuring that everyone is balanced during such madness is key.

Give your all both to the sport you play and to your academic foundation; this will not only support your efforts as a student-athlete, but it will also support you long after your academic and athletic days are over.

The goal of playing professional sports never faded for me in college, nor should it for you if that's your goal. I'll be the first to tell anyone: never give up on your dreams. Just remember that you're continuously evolving over the years, and so will your goals. Strive for a balance, to position yourself for success. That way, whatever happens, you're tooled for success.

Many of you reading this book have aspirations or will develop an aspiration to play professional sports. Many know of someone who has this target drawn into their future. No matter the sport, league or stage of life, dreams are a powerful force which can indeed produce powerful results. Just remember to take advantage of where you currently are by understanding what your priorities are—especially what matters most to you and allows your dreams to come closer.

And that's how you navigate the insanity.

FOLLOW-UP QUESTIONS

1. What is your ultimate dream? What is your present goal to achieve that ultimate dream?

2. Evaluate your current situation for ways to develop balance. List some distractions, or just activities that aren't productive during this phase of your life. What activities or poor habits can you eliminate?

3. Rather than focusing on what you don't have, what do you have? How can you maximize your available resources?

CHAPTER 2

Expand Your View

Student-athletes have to be adaptive creatures: our teammates change; our coaches change; we play for different teams. We compete on our high-school teams, go with travel teams and attend local and international camps. On the college level, we play known teams within our conference and out-of-conference teams we're unaccustomed to. Then March Madness, bowl games and tournament season roll around, and we must adapt and be ready to go up against some of the world's greatest competitors.

I remember the beginning of my freshman year at Georgetown and having to rapidly adapt to the pace of the season. Every game presented a very different challenge, and the competition continued to improve. We'd prepare intensively for an opponent that had a dominant point guard. Our entire defensive strategy would be to contain this one player and disrupt the other team's tempo. Once the buzzer sounded, at the next practice (or sometimes even on the drive back to DC) we were watching scouting film on our next opponent. And they were extremely different.

Thousands of student-athletes arrive at colleges, large and small, public and private institutions around the country each year, and they are armed with the athletic talent and drive that afforded them a full scholarship or a partial athletic scholarship. There are many who aren't on scholarship, but they are extremely talented and are just as important to their teams. Regardless of your path to college, once you arrive, be prepared to expand your view—be very prepared.

Truth is, countless numbers of student-athletes arrive unprepared to handle the academic rigors of the college experience, making it almost impossible to capitalize on the opportunity that sits before them.

Well, how do you ensure that you arrive at college prepared?

STEP ONE: TAKE THE WHEEL: IT'S YOUR JOURNEY

The bright lights of high-school and college athletics—the massive crowds, the adoration from fellow students, the support of alumni and the attraction that many have for the billion-dollar sporting industry—can fog the focus of the best of us. In fact, all the accolades you can get from people who see you as someone who has succeeded beyond their wildest dreams can distract you from figuring out what you really want from college and how to obtain it. And there's more out there than you think. You have to look beyond the bright lights and hunt for the resources that are afforded to you as a student-athlete.

This is your career, and you owe it to yourself to have a panoramic view of your possibilities; don't leave that to anyone else. It is easy to get sucked into the vacuum of college athletics, which isn't necessarily a bad thing . . . unless athletics is all that's in there. Some people will see you as an athlete first (some will see you as "just" an athlete), and this label can get you what some may view as special treatment. I can remember a fellow student saying, "Don't worry about the group assignment; we'll take care of it. I know you have a rigorous preparation schedule—it's almost Big East tournament time." It was a kind gesture, but don't allow others to do your job or make your role easier. These can be defining moments—never accept any special treatment that isn't of high ethical standards or which is against university and/or NCAA rules and regulations. Trust me, it isn't worth it.

I went on two official college visits, and Georgetown was my second. All through the first visit, I already knew that Georgetown had my heart, and there was no changing that—I wanted to be a Hoya. But something happened during the first college tour that made my decision that much easier.

My first cousin, who was more like a little brother to me, dropped me off at the Memphis airport. I felt weird because he and I had dreamed of attending the same college, just as we were attending the same high school. In college, we'd be a one-two punch, and from there we'd both play in the NBA. Even if one of us didn't make it that far, we would ensure the other was fully included in the experience. I boarded the plane with my SAT prep book in hand, and while I looked forward to the experience, something felt off.

At my destination, one of the assistant coaches greeted me with high energy, which was reassuring. We walked together to the baggage claim and then to his car. When we passed through the airport-parking tollbooth, he paid the attendant, then casually passed me what he called "the change"—it was a hundred and sixty dollars. As a high-school senior from inner-city Memphis, Tennessee, that was a lot of money. I was so stunned and confused by the gesture that I took it.

After a weekend on campus hanging out with the team and a very gracious outing for the entire team to the head coach's house, I had had a great time—yet the money weighed on me. I knew it was wrong. On our way back to the airport, I handed the money back to the coach and told him that I could not accept it, but thanks anyway. I knew it wasn't the school for me.

Your athletic career is just that: yours. DO NOT allow someone and their unethical practices and/or decisions to cloud your actions. Know the rules.

And if you aren't sure, ask.

When I started at Georgetown, my view of myself was limited to what others thought I should do. If it involved academics, I relied primarily on the counsel of others; if someone said a course was easy, I'd take it. I directed my attention toward suggestions such as which majors were the least challenging and which professors were more "understanding" of the rigors of the student-athlete lifestyle. Getting by was the only thing that mattered. I had no problem taking the easy road, just so I would have more time to focus on basketball.

By my junior year, I was on a different track. I realized what I had in front of me, and I wasn't going to let it slip away. I vividly remember being excited to prove myself at Georgetown, both academically and athletically. It was my journey, so I took the wheel. That was when I started to become a true student-athlete—and an **Athlete for Life**.

STEP TWO: COME PREPARED

When game day rolls around, you've practiced hard for facing your opponent. You and your teammates and coaches have invested countless hours of preparation, conditioning and applying mental focus to accomplish the mission.

Once I took the wheel of my journey, I applied this same framework to my academics.

When meeting with my coaches and academic adviser to discuss academics, I came to the meetings prepared. I approached these meetings as if they were a game. I came with questions and a list of courses that I wanted to take based on my interests.

Were they surprised? Yes! It was almost as if I were a different person. I could tell they were surprised, but I heard the relief in their voices and saw their expressions—their reactions might have been *Great, I don't have to worry about Omari anymore—he's got it.*

Just remember that in life, preparation is highly respected. There will be times when you prepare for an opponent or project and don't receive a favorable result—yet when you put forth the work and your best effort, there is a calmness and a confidence you'll feel inside because you applied yourself.

STEP 3: UNDERSTAND YOU ARE AN AMBASSADOR FOR YOUR UNIVERSITY: RESPECT IS MUTUAL

Colleges are primarily composed of professors, administration and students. It sounds simple, but let me break it down.

Professors are the academic leaders. Through hands-on experience and in-depth research, they lead discussions that direct and influence policy in their respective fields domestically and internationally. They maintain a level of expertise, executive leadership and service within their educational institution, whether it be leading a foreign-expansion advisory committee or investing time and research into an academic text or methodology that can be studied by future leaders at colleges and universities all over the world.

I signed my first adjunct-faculty agreement at Georgetown University in 2015. Through my experiences as a cultural envoy and diplomat for the US Department of State, I developed a course called Sport, Culture and Diplomacy. This field changed my life, and I knew more about the subject than anyone I knew. So I thought I should create my own course and teach it. I was truly a subject-matter expert in a niche area. I presented my course ideas to Georgetown, and they jumped at the course. It was an honor to teach at the university that had taught me so much.

Standing in front of my students for the very first time brought me back to my days as a student. I realized that I was the one to challenge, teach and, most importantly, listen. I had crossed over, which was just weird. But I loved it and still love it to this day. Standing before a group of eager master's-level students was a rush, and it still is.

Academic institutions recruit, and fight to retain, professors, global thinkers and educational administrators who in turn attract bright students, challenge their minds to solve problems and develop innovative avenues to address today's tasks. Ask anyone outside the United States where they want to attend college and they are more than likely going to pick someplace in the United States.

Many student-athletes are heavily recruited; some fall into the lifestyle while at college by trying out for the team and becoming walk-ons. While everyone's journey may be different, the effort required to be at the top of your game is the same.

To have college coaches write letters, show up at your front door, sit in your living room and pitch why their university is best for your future—that's an incredible gesture and reaffirms how special you and your skill set are.

It's similar with professors: they are at the top of their field, and that's why they are trusted to guide you through a learning process. They respect the effort you put in as a student-athlete. They know it isn't easy. They know you represent the school just as they do. Get to know them as best as you can, and you will realize that you have more in common than you ever imagined.

STEP 4: FLY LIKE AN EAGLE

If you arrive at college solely focused on succeeding in sports, you are cutting your potential short. Let me provide a metaphor.

The American bald eagle is a global symbol of freedom and strength. This incredible creature can have a six-foot wingspan and can fly up to ten thousand feet. When hunting, it can spot prey from over a mile away and strike it by diving at a speed of over a hundred miles per hour.

How do you think eagles learn to do that? By watching their parents, then by jumping from branch to branch near their nests. If you take a young eaglet and raise it among chickens, the eagle will never reach its full capabilities. It only knows what it sees.

During my freshman and sophomore years in

college, I struggled to gain traction both academically and athletically—mostly due to placing basketball first and making everything else secondary, a bad habit I developed over time. I had received the proper instructions from others who really cared, yet the wisdom never translated to me because my sports journey was so unusual in my family and among anyone I had ever played with—or at least that was how I perceived it at the time. Therefore, I internalized a lot and listened only to myself (we will explore this further in Chapter 8). The people you love and trust are in your life for a reason; a resource such as this book and others offers valuable knowledge from lessons learned.

Your life is your own journey, but you don't have to travel it alone.

Truth is, just as I began to contemplate giving up on my Georgetown University dream and goal, those natural athletic instincts began to take full effect—no quitting; work hard, then work harder; remember the bigger picture; consider what matters most to me and what will define my legacy. I thought of all these lessons. I learned them from watching my parents and listening to my coaches over time, and these were the basic principles I learned and applied to my sports journey.

I expanded my view, which led to unleashing my potential. I began to fly.

THIS IS YOUR OPPORTUNITY

If you arrive at your college campus preparing to succeed only at your sport and seeing class as secondary, you cut yourself and your future short. Come prepared to spread your wings and glide to your fullest potential. Expand your view, and know that you can be a great player in basketball, field hockey, track, lacrosse or football and also a major contributor to the academic community. You can triumph at both; it just takes effort to have the will to capitalize on the full college experience and the confidence not to bend to society's expectation of what you are capable of achieving.

As an athlete, you've been proving people wrong all your life: don't stop when you get to the classroom. By expanding your view, you can analyze and comprehend the full picture, allowing you to completely prepare and adapt to new environments, unfamiliar situations and the myriad transitions which are all part of life.

FOLLOW-UP QUESTIONS

1. What comes easy to you? What's a real challenge to pick up? Answer these questions both for academics and athletics.

2. What can you do to make your strengths truly world-class?

3. What can you do to make your weaknesses not just average, but real strengths?

CHAPTER 3

Managing Time

THE PHONE CALL

Midway through my sophomore year, my mother called me with that tone in her voice—the one where you know something's wrong. I immediately thought the worst—someone had passed away or been badly hurt. But it turned out I was the one causing her stress.

"One of your coaches called," she said. "He said you are close to being academically ineligible"—my heart sank to my knees—"and you could lose your athletic scholarship." I never wanted to provoke that tone of voice from my mother again.

There were a lot of reasons my mother received that phone call, but along with my skewed priorities (which I'll get to later), the other big issue was my lack of time management.

NEXT LEVEL

You may have thought high school was a busy time, but college is another thing altogether. You have a lot more things to get done, both academically and athletically, and you also have to build a whole new social network around yourself. But you still have the same number of minutes and hours in a day to do all of this as you had before. Don't allow yourself to waste time while in college, because once the opportunity is over, you can't get it back.

Think of your time as a vital nutrient to your life, just like water. Just imagine: you and your teammates are on an island, and one of your responsibilities is to transport water from the ocean to base camp. To do so, you have two options: use a solid and sturdy bucket or one with holes in the bottom. Why would anyone want to use a bucket that merely allows water to fall out the bottom?

The same scenario applies when managing your time. You don't want to manage it improperly, and you don't want important priorities to fall through the cracks.

In college, if a major exam or paper falls through the cracks, that can not only affect your grade but also your eligibility, not to mention the trust and credibility that you have with your teachers, teammates and fellow students. Once that credibility is lost, it can be impossible to regain. Truth is, you are different; your workload is unique, and the value you will bring to your university is priceless. Being a student-athlete takes work, extra effort and prioritization.

There will be times when you need an extension on a deadline, and it is during these moments that the credibility you have developed comes into account. As a professor, I know my students and am always willing to accommodate a student with a special case that doesn't allow them to turn in an assignment on time. While being a student-athlete is a special case, it doesn't call for you to be late for class, miss assignments regularly, not be present for group assignments, etc. These are all signs of lack of prioritizing and time management.

I have seen teammates work hard every day in practice and in games and become major pieces to a team's success, only to be declared academically ineligible. And if you miss games because you're on academic probation, it can affect the trust you have with the rest of your team.

I had problems managing my time, and it's still not easy, but it is necessary. Here's the method that got me through.

WRITE THIS DOWN

Being a student-athlete taught me that I had to do multiple things at once and even sometimes be multiple places at once (believe me, it's possible). The way I turned my time management around wasn't complicated—I used a prioritizing methodology.

That's a fancy way of saying *I wrote stuff down*.

I figured out my short-term and long-term deliverables and ranked them every week. For example, in class the near-term deliverables might include posting comments in an online-class discussion, papers that are due, group-assignment commitments and reading books and articles, etc. The long-term deliverables are something along the lines of graduating with honors and being ready for the world that awaits, retaining the lessons you've learned and applying those theories to your everyday life and challenging yourself to be a contributing member of the university community for years to come.

Knowing your athletics deliverables is equally important. Near-term deliverables could be learning the defensive-offensive sets, weight-room strength and conditioning, training-room treatments for injuries and attentiveness during film sessions (which, again, is on a whole different level in college). The long-term deliverables could include becoming a mentor to freshman and sophomore members of the team, becoming a captain and, most importantly, reaching your full potential as an athlete, applying the theories of sports to your everyday life and challenging yourself as an **Athlete for Life**. Delivering isn't always easy, but writing down your short- and long-term deliverables will pay off in the future.

At first, I used Post-it notes on a wall—that's easy to rearrange as you change the order of priorities. Then I started using my version of the

Franklin Covey system (a paper-based time-management system created by Hyrum W. Smith—the system's name references Benjamin Franklin, who was known to keep a small, very detailed journal to track daily events). It classifies tasks as Important and Urgent, Important but Not Urgent, Not Important but Urgent and Not Important and Not Urgent. The important thing is to put it in writing.

At first, I resisted doing that, for a couple of reasons. First, I thought I shouldn't have to write everything down—I should be able to remember everything. After all, I always had. But like I said, there's so much more to keep track of in college. Second, whenever I had to change the order of my deliverables, it made me feel like the whole system wasn't working. But that's not what it means.

During my junior year at Georgetown, our coaches implemented a new zone defense called *the wheel*. This defensive adjustment changed our habitual approach, and the modification came in the middle of the season, at a time when it should have been all about perfecting the existing defenses. Our coaches drilled us with urgency—it was the same defense Georgetown played in the 1982 NCAA championship game against the North Carolina Tar Heels. In that game, a broken-down Georgetown defensive rotation in the final minute allowed a young Tar Heel freshman to hit a baseline jump shot, effectively ending Georgetown's championship journey and beginning what we now know as a legendary sports career. That young freshman was Michael Jordan.

Managing Time

Most of our coaches were either coaches or players on that 1982 Georgetown team, and believe me, once you get that close to winning you never forget. So we were drilled and pushed to perfect our defense so that result would never happen again.

But as an upperclassman, I quickly saw that we were not adjusting effectively to this new defense. It was a disaster the first couple of weeks. During games, our team looked confused and disorganized when we switched to the new defense. Still, we never wavered.

Our coaches were committed to the defense, and in due time, so were we. We improved, and so did our confidence in the defense. It took practice and commitment, and so will any time-management system you choose to implement. It will take work, and it may not seem to work in the beginning, but it can prove to be a valuable tool that will propel you throughout your life. It takes time to learn new plays or sets, or to find the real secrets buried in game film, and it takes time to list your deliverables in the right order. When you have to change up your list because something is more or less important than you first realized, that's all it means. There is nothing wrong with finding you need to rearrange your priorities.

When you write your deliverables down, you know when you don't deliver on something—it stares you right in the face. And you're going to be surprised at how good it feels to actually—physically—cross something off the list. You did it—now it's done, and on you go to the next!

And one other thing you'll soon see: writing all your deliverables down makes the job look smaller. Trust me; it never, ever looks as big on paper as it seems in your head. Once it is written down, you have a full view of your action items; when you store everything in your mind, you tend to prioritize mentally, which often places a priority on the deliverables that are most immediate. Tasks that may seem minor, because they are weeks or months away, can be forgotten or neglected. Allowing these habits to settle in can become problematic during your college years and will impact your ability to succeed on and off the court.

FREEDOM

One of the good things about your new situation is that you do have a bit of leeway on how exactly you get things done.

I once took a public-speaking class, and I needed to do a forty-five-minute keynote address as a project. It was due in the middle of the season, and I knew I wasn't going to have a lot of time at the last minute. So I would often write and practice on the road by myself, and with a small recorder, I'd work on my speech during breaks and finish the rest at night.

You have to improvise sometimes, but once you know the goal, you'll be ready. And it's a good feeling going into that final project not having crammed everything at the last second.

THE SECRET TO TIME MANAGEMENT

Making a list also helps you with one of the dirty secrets both of college and of adulthood: how to confidently say NO.

Saying yes is easy. Saying yes gives you that immediate gratification, that immediate admiration from others, which can become addictive. It can overwhelm your good sense. But saying yes to things means saying no to others—whether you mean to or not.

Early on, whatever was thrown my way, I said yes to everything. But that can lead to feeling overwhelmed by deliverables. One of the important steps toward good time management is looking at your list of deliverables, which you have written down, to see whether you can get something done—and if you can't, realizing that and not agreeing to it in the first place. You might think the person you're turning down will be upset, but they'll be a whole lot more upset if you tell them you'll deliver and then you don't.

I vividly remember days in high school when I had many academic priorities that were key, such as final papers, exams and extremely important tasks such as studying for the ACT and SAT exams. But I looked up to my youngest uncle, Darrell, my older cousins and my big brother, all of whom were amazing basketball players. They were the true definition of basketball junkies and gym rats. On weekends, when they'd say, "Want to go hoop?" or "Let's go to the gym and put up a few hundred shots" (which would easily turn into a few thousand), I would almost always say yes—not because I always wanted to but because I didn't want to disappoint them. I wanted them to know I was committed to being the best basketball player.

I got away with that in high school, but I couldn't do it in college. Today, I understand that being the best basketball player includes the moments when you have to say no to athletic activities to leave the time to invest in your studies.

The second half of my college academic career was more productive because I realized the value of saying no. It's tough in the beginning because you have required courses that you'd say no to if you could. But it gets better once you realize what you academically enjoy most: I learned I liked to write and speak, so taking English classes, for example, became a natural choice for me. And by then I knew how much I could accomplish, and I didn't take on any more than I could handle.

CONTINUAL PROGRESS

Your personal time-management strategy becomes yours to keep. It will be easier to apply this strategy once you transition from college to your professional career path, whether the next step is a professional athletic career or creating a start-up. If you can organize your time effectively, it will pay off tremendously. I have had many of my teammates and friends go on to play professionally in a variety of sports, and the one point that remains consistent is their focus on the importance of time management.

In my last year at Georgetown, a lot of my classmates were kicking back, enjoying senior year; some were stressed and overwhelmed by the next phase of life. I was extremely busy scheduling interviews, being a senior leader on the team and going to career-networking events. I completed each task with ease because I had a defined, proven time-management system that worked for me.

And now my days are jam-packed with new priorities: volunteering, kids' sports activities, nonprofit meetings, messaging and brainstorming sessions, PTO events, state advisory-board meetings, Navy Reserve duty, speaking engagements, writing articles and books and more. But as a true **Athlete for Life**, I still keep it all straight by prioritizing—by writing it all down. Many ask, *How do you keep it all together so easily?* My response: *it's not always easy, but I'm an* **Athlete for Life**. *It's just what we do!*

FOLLOW-UP QUESTIONS

1. Evaluate your priorities and list them in order. Now make a list of the things you actually spend most of your day doing. Which priorities need to be shifted? Make a list and categorize into three buckets (high, medium, low) to help organize your current time management.

2. What are your academic and athletic deliverables, both near-term and long-term? For the week, month and semester? Write them down, then rank every week.

3. Zone in on your current priorities listed above. How have your priorities shifted since transitioning from high school to college?

CHAPTER 4

Take Control of Your Message

We are connected more than ever, and as methods of communication continue to evolve, student-athletes must quickly and frequently adjust to new norms.

Whether you are a five-star recruit or a skilled athlete looking to make your school's team as a walk-on, communication today allows the competition pool to increase dramatically, and that is why your message counts. College coaches now have direct access to databases with tens of thousands of players ranked by hundreds of reliable (and some not so reliable) sources, all at their fingertips. That expands the competition pool significantly.

Communication and connectivity allow a sports analyst to watch game film of a player in

Texas, write a hundred-and-fifty-word blog about their strengths and weaknesses, speculate which colleges are recruiting them and add any other gossip that can be found on or off the internet—a blog, a tweet, word of mouth or sometimes simply speculation. They can click on publish from their laptop or phone while seated at a sixteen-and-under Euro League tournament in Spain, sending a message to hundreds of thousands within seconds. That message is there; you can read it, but you can't change it.

The power of communication today is stronger than it's ever been, and it will only get stronger with time.

Understanding the flow of information and communication and your role in the process of creating your image and your message will lead to a competitive edge both on and off the field. Once you master this key element, you place yourself at a competitive advantage—you are now in the driver's seat. Unlike in a game situation, you're not looking your competition directly in the eyes, but the same approach and preparation is critical to cultivating a personal package that no college program—or post-college opportunity—would want to say no to.

You have the opportunity to create a brand image for yourself which will work for you the rest of your life.

YOU AND YOUR ACTIONS

Your message is like a business card: it provides those who don't have regular access to you a preview of the person, the student and the athlete you are. You project your message when you're walking around school, stepping off the team bus or appearing on a YouTube video, and it provides people insight about you. So you need to control that message and take care of that which is within your control: yourself and your actions.

When I began my college career at Georgetown University, only one other full-scholarship basketball player from Memphis had played for the Hoyas since the early 1990s. That player went on to develop bitter feelings regarding his college experience and would later stalk then-head coach John Thompson, which resulted in a court order to stay away from the Georgetown campus. Let's just say that Memphis prospects weren't high on the list of Georgetown basketball recruiting!

But the summer before my freshman year in high school, I attended a basketball camp—my messaging, communication and a little luck may have later changed the Georgetown coaching staff's mind about Memphis prospects, and their open-mindedness changed my life.

Hosted in Memphis, the program was called the Tick Price Basketball Camp. Tick Price was then the head coach for the University of Memphis. Since I lived in Brunswick, Georgia, with my mom and had grown almost five inches in the previous eighteen months, no one knew who I was.

I was just myself, a kid visiting his hometown for the summer and looking to play basketball. I played hard, but I was nervous in such a new environment.

— ATHLETE FOR LIFE —

Still, I even surprised myself; I'd come a long way in a short time. I had improved athletically, and my confidence in my own abilities was much stronger.

I won the MVP award at the camp that summer, and I will never forget one coach who was there. His name was Chip Simms, and he left his mark on me, though I wouldn't fully understand this impact until years later.

Coach Simms was then an assistant coach at the University of Memphis. Almost all Division I, II and III programs host college summer camps for youth sports. This isn't considered recruiting, but I'm sure if a coach sees a standout talent, they just might take note and remain in touch, or even recommend that their counterparts at other universities take note.

Coach Simms left the University of Memphis a few years later and soon began recruiting me once he returned to his alma mater, Georgetown University, as an assistant coach.

At Georgetown, I struggled the summer before my sophomore year. I was bitter and thought I should have gotten more playing time the year before. Coach Simms pulled me aside one afternoon and said, "You need to tap into the kid I knew that summer in Memphis—you walked into the camp as a confident champion! So pick yourself up. Carry yourself like that kid I first saw who no one knew."

I needed that wake-up call.

Coach Simms passed away unexpectedly in 2016; he was only forty-six. I am forever appreciative about how I carried myself that summer at the Tick Price camp. While everything was new and overwhelming, I projected the image of what I wanted to become—a champion.

Thanks, Coach Simms. Be well among the angels.

You can't control what anyone writes about you or how they choose to rank you against your peers, but you can control your own actions—the ones that create your personal message. Pay close attention to three factors: your network, how you carry yourself and what you post. These factors are all in your control, and they'll create your own personal message.

YOUR NETWORK

Your network consists of your closest and trusted advisers: your brothers and sisters, a hometown friend, parents, teammates, girlfriends and boyfriends, AAU coaches, etc.

Maybe your little sister studies the game in and out and provides you with positive and negative feedback on how you played in the second half; maybe you and a teammate at your position both find value working together outside of practice, studying together or doing things outside of sports; your AAU coach might be your go-to on matters such as upcoming training camps, tournaments, etc. These relationships can be fruitful in many ways and can last your whole life.

During my senior year at Georgetown, one of my teammates completed an internship at the Department of State. He enjoyed the experience beyond measure, and after workouts, I would pepper him with questions. I had grown a lot since my freshman year, and international affairs was beginning to be a huge interest. This was post 9/11, therefore I plugged myself into everything which happened on a global stage, and I enjoyed seeing him experience an amazing internship.

One day after practice in mid-November, he asked me whether I'd like to join him for Thanksgiving dinner at the home of the gentleman he had interned with the past summer. For basketball players, the campus was like a ghost town during the Thanksgiving holiday. While almost all the students, administration and faculty had left to enjoy the holiday with family and or friends, we athletes were cooped up on campus, practicing and preparing for Coastal Carolina and Delaware State that year. So when he asked me to have dinner at a home with family, even if it wasn't my family, I jumped at it.

This Thanksgiving was one of the most memorable experiences of my senior year, and having the opportunity to meet someone who, in my opinion, served our country with honor and distinction was motivating. It also reinforced for me that the subject of international affairs was of importance to me, and I wanted to experience more. Years later, I established a relationship with my teammate's internship manager, and today I consider him a mentor and one of the finest examples of service to others. Today, my teammate and I remain in contact too. Our wives and children have met each other, and I consider him a man of great integrity, a friend and always my teammate. He remains a part of my network and always will.

Those kinds of opportunities happen all the time, and you need to be open to them (as I mention in Chapter 2, Expand Your View). Just make sure that your network comprises people who represent you now and positively project the future you are working toward: be sure they are enhancements to your personal message.

Once, early in my college years, basketball wasn't turning out as I had envisioned it, and I spent too much time with the wrong people at Georgetown. In my eyes, my situation was deteriorating, and that led to an *I don't care* attitude. Even when I returned home to Memphis for short breaks, I engaged in risky behavior and activities that could have been extremely damaging to my future. I placed myself in compromising situations.

While I didn't break any laws, certain crowds and activities were a part of my life then, even though they were not representative of what I was or who I wanted to be, nor were they anything I should have been associated with.

I missed my family and hanging out with my friends—some of them, anyway. Finally, during these breaks, I had to make some very difficult decisions about who I could hang out with and who could possibly cause long-term damage to my future. Some of my former friends and teammates had begun to dabble in selling drugs and associating with the type of crowd that usually draws—things had changed significantly. On school breaks, I could no longer risk being pulled over in a car that had illegal drugs and guns in it.

Former Hamilton High School standout and current Georgetown basketball hoop star arrested for guns and drugs—not the headline I could afford to have associated with my personal message.

HEADLINE CRAFTING

The truth is that you absolutely can't craft the headline for a story you aren't writing, nor should you drive yourself senseless trying to craft a headline for someone else's story. What you can do is control the content that you provide others to write about.

You have to be conscious of the headline. Headlines don't always tell the whole story, and sometimes they are misleading, false or just plain wrong, but often there can be some truth to these bold titles. The morning after a game in my senior year in high school, I remember picking up the newspaper, and the headline read, *Faulkner carries Hamilton Wildcats by city rival East High.* I thought, *Really?* I had had a great fourth quarter but a disastrous first half, and my teammates carried the load until I finally found my rhythm and we closed the deal.

To whoever wrote that article and those who read the headlines, it appeared I was the savior and carried our team to victory. This was a case where a headline made me look good yet didn't tell the full story, but you can't count on anyone telling your full story but you. Just consider: *if someone were to take one fact out of this narrative, what would it be?* You can see it doesn't take much for something to make you look bad or good—and to interfere with the creation of your personal message.

Truth be told, everyone has their own journey in life. I didn't judge my old teammates for their decisions. Some judged me for not being able to ride in the same cars and attend the same parties as I used to, but some of them understood then, and they understand now, and they remain my good friends today. Don't be afraid to be honest. As athletes, we work hard at our craft, we seek to be the best at what we do and therefore we have a lot to lose, so we go the extra mile. Be proud to be in that situation, make your own headlines and take inventory of your network.

CARRYING YOURSELF

Be mindful of how you carry yourself. Sounds like something a grandparent would say, right? Well, it is. I spent a lot of weekends with my great-grandmother, who was a community leader, the heartbeat of our family and a devout Christian. On Saturdays, she would have someone come over and give all the boys what she called *college cuts*. I never knew what this meant—just that I couldn't get a cool haircut like any of the styles I saw on TV and in magazines. The college cut was stubble-low and even all around. Knowing we were going to church the next day, she'd say to us, "You go to God's house looking your best," and tell the barber, "Give them the look of those good college boys."

My aunt later told me that she had dated a

young man in her younger years who had aspirations of going to college. Back in those days, that was almost unfathomable for a young black man, but she remembered how well-groomed he was and how he spoke and carried himself—like a young man who was going to college, who had the dreams and ambitions of someone on the move. I wonder to this day whether he ever got that opportunity—the opportunity you have now.

The definition of *how you carry yourself* is simple: if you care, show you care. We have all heard the saying *you can't judge a book by its cover*. Well, you can't judge whether it's any good by its cover, but you can probably tell what it's about. What would your story be about? When people are discussing your book two days or twenty years from now, what would you like them to remember?

How you carry yourself isn't about being something you're not. It's the opposite—it's the best of who you really are, where you want to be and the effort it takes to get there.

Midway through college, I was still dressing like I had in high school, when I wanted nothing more than to be recognized as a basketball player. One day, I had had enough—I had changed my outlook on my purpose; I was a different person, and I wanted to look like it. I wanted to try something different, and I transformed the way I dressed, and it felt good.

I didn't stop there. I sought other ways to improve.

I recognized that I lacked public-speaking skills.

I wasn't comfortable speaking in class because of my deep Southern accent; some people literally couldn't understand the words coming out of my mouth. My first year, I stayed in a shell and didn't care whether they heard me or not.

Then I realized that was only hurting me, so I decided to change that as part of how I carried myself. I read aloud in my room almost every night and became more comfortable with my speech and the correct pronunciation of words. Today, I love public speaking and enjoy the power of direct communication with crowds large and small. Most of all, I love reading to my daughters—it reminds me of my days of reading aloud by myself. But now I have an attentive audience!

Be mindful of you, yourself and your situation. Be sure you are representing the person you've become and the positive values that are woven into your personal fabric today—and align your actions of the present with your visions of the future.

WHAT YOU POST

Social media was in its infancy during my college years, but today it is a major form of communication and messaging.

Some may believe that student-athletes should restrict their use of social media, while others promote its usage for branding purposes. I see social media as a terrific way to connect with people, groups and cultures all over the world. You can track the news, engage with other students and student-athletes at other colleges and have yet another opportunity to control your own message and be yourself.

My advice is simple. Social media isn't for everyone, nor does it have to be. If you find social media enjoyable and beneficial to you, you should embrace it. Yet remember, it's not what you do, it's how you do it—anything positive can become a negative force, depending on the user and/or its implementation.

Whatever you post sticks with you—always remember that. You can delete something, but it never goes completely away, especially if someone takes a screenshot of what you posted. Social media is a great tool for college recruiting, and you can and should let your social-media activity represent the person you are. But remember: What would you want a college coach to take away from viewing your social-media feeds? What will a future employer think about your selection of posts? You control that message, no one else does.

After college, when you join the professional ranks, even if you are playing a sport professionally, your social-media presence can have an impact. Employers have recruiting departments solely dedicated to finding out as much information as possible about someone before making an investment in hiring them. This is true of professional sports, summer internships and entry-level positions in most fields.

Social media is also an avenue for those looking for influence on a student-athlete or direct access to the team. Inappropriate usages of social media—in either direction—could have a lasting impact on your future, jeopardize your NCAA eligibility standing and cause a distraction for your team, so be wise in how and with whom you engage.

Social media is great and dangerous, both for the same reason—you own it. Be yourself, but watch what type of message you are presenting.

PEOPLE TO PEOPLE

When you are seeking to fully understand and connect with someone, the most effective method of communication will be centered on people-to-people interactions. Technology innovations continue to advance and become more and more involved in how we communicate, yet there is still no substitute for in-person, eye-to-eye communication. When you are in the heat of athletic competition, it's just you, your teammates and opponents. There are no phones, pads, tablets, computers, etc.; therefore, you must remember to place a priority on person-to-person interactions, as they are the fuel for communication and connection.

Months after my college graduation, I traveled to Bosnia and Herzegovina. This was my first trip outside the United States. The moment I arrived in Sarajevo, everything looked and felt different. I was adjusting to the time zone in Eastern Europe, the language barrier, the climate and the dramatic cultural differences. While walking around, people would just stare at me, not in a rude way but almost in amazement. One lady I met at my hotel, who had spent ten years studying in the United States, said directly, "Most people in this city haven't seen black Americans, so get used to it." And I did.

While everything was different and unfamiliar to me, my very first basketball clinic in Bosnia was a smash hit! None of the coaches or youth participants spoke English, but we all knew and enjoyed basketball—it was the connector. We laughed, we played and most importantly, we learned from each other. Some even cried toward the end of our time together. Today, sports diplomacy remains an effective interactive tool within the international diplomacy arena, and while connecting people through different channels such as digital diplomacy has become more popular, ask anyone: nothing can replace in-person communication. It is powerful.

COMMUNICATION CHALLENGE

I challenge you to spend more time connecting directly with your parents, coaches, neighbors, teammates, etc. Put aside your phone for a moment, and fully focus on the interaction. I guarantee you will notice a dramatic difference.

Your message is crafted and created by you, your actions and how you communicate. The growth and development of your communication skills, as that relates to conveying your message, will continue to progress over time, but in order to progress, you have to practice. Remain cognizant that you are the driver of your personal message—no one else.

FOLLOW-UP QUESTIONS

1. Think about your personal business card. How would you convey your personal brand/message within 30 seconds?

2. List three attributes/areas you admire about yourself that you would want someone to think of when they hear your name, and then list three things you wouldn't want associated with your name.

3. Your life is a story and as you mature and become an adult you assume the leading role in directing your story. Ask yourself often—how am I controlling my message? What is my story about?

CHAPTER 5

Find Your Music

THE TUNE: COMMUTING TO THE GAME

Our team commuted to our home games from our sleepy Georgetown campus to the bustling streets of downtown DC. We'd pass by the Washington Monument, the Lincoln Memorial and the White House. Sometimes I'd look through the bus window and take it all in—the tourists (they were the ones walking aimlessly) and the everyday Washington dwellers (they would stride aggressively, yet with poise and purpose).

Many times I barely saw anything on the commutes from campus to the MCI Center, now known as the Capital One Arena. Sometimes I'd close my eyes and just relax, daydream, write in my journal or just nap. Regardless of whether my eyes were open or closed, I could feel the presence of the people walking along and taking pictures by the monuments and the scores of fans piling into the arena.

I knew it was time to get moving when I saw the bustle of Chinatown and the arena staff moving hastily, hard at work preparing for our arrival and the thousands of fans. The bomb-sniffing dogs were always a comforting sight and a continual reminder of the security threats of the post 9/11 era. The dogs always seemed eager to play their role and that always made me feel safe. These sights and sounds were all a part of my music.

There's no one definition of *music* in this context, because it means something different to us all. Music is something YOU feel deep inside; it's personal, and once you feel music that's yours, you just know it. If a globally respected philosopher told you that the tune that makes your heart dance wasn't music—you'd probably look that person right back in the eye and confidently say, *Yeah, right!*

You will not be the first student-athlete at your school; there have been tens of thousands, maybe even hundreds of thousands, before you. But no two journeys are the same, and you have to work toward the establishment of your very own legacy. Just imagine if Beethoven had never challenged the cultural norms of music, or if Aretha Franklin had thought that her voice wasn't as lovely as those before her. What if Michael Jackson had never thought to move the needle of entertainment to the next level? What if Ray Charles had believed that a blind person had no role in music? All these respected musicians had previous examples of greatness, yet they each carved a new pathway. Your music will be different from the next person's.

GAME TIME

Whether it was an exhibition game with three thousand in attendance or a Big East Conference duel with twenty-thousand-plus screaming fans, the energy and environment of a game, and my connection to it, felt surreal. As still as a three-hundred-year-old painting, these moments created memories that are forever enshrined in my heart. They are my tune, my beat—my music.

These lasting memories varied, from the sound of music blasting through the speakers while running onto our shiny, professionally buffed Georgetown arena floor to the vibrations of our high-school band blasting their brass instruments while we sprinted onto our worn gym floor just a few hours after we'd played dodgeball in PE on the same surface. My heart would pound in my chest so loudly it felt as though it were dancing. Even during away games I'd feel the same, but there is never any place like home.

It didn't even matter too much what the music was; I'd burst from the tunnel as if I were running to the music, and in that moment, the nervousness subsided. In that moment was where I found the most enjoyment, underneath the bright lights, my heart pounding like a drum through the

Georgetown jersey on my chest. It was my moment.

YOUR ACADEMIC TUNE

As a student-athlete, once you set foot on a college campus, or even as early as middle school and high school, it's important to define your academic tune.

So how do you do it? First, approach your first day in college as an opportunity to listen to the music you love for the rest of your college experience, and ask yourself: What are the academic subjects that open your ears? What areas of study do you wish to learn more about? What subjects are you already good at? Where do you hear the music?

Once you ask yourself these important questions and establish the answers, your academic tune will be set. That will bring balance to your academic environment, and this maturation will allow you to progress academically and athletically.

College isn't easy, but the sooner you find the tune that drives you to take action, the sooner you'll be able to compete among the best athletic talent and compete against the best students in class. Soon you may realize that you are one of those top students yourself.

Obstacles don't have to stop you. If you run into a wall, don't turn around and give up. Figure out how to climb it, go through it, or work around it.
—Michael Jordan

That moment I found my academic tune at Georgetown was the moment I lifted myself from being an athlete who attended a university to a student-athlete uplifting the university. As it relates to academics, finding your music isn't as hard as you'd imagine:

Start Early: *Connect your academic interest to your future growth and development potential.*

The second semester of my sophomore year, I had to face the music: my grades were failing miserably, and I hated going to class. I oftentimes felt like a fish out of water, like I didn't belong, and honestly, my focus was off balance. Basketball consumed me. I had two choices: throw in the towel on my current situation by transferring to another school, just head back home or find my music—open my eyes and ears, and listen to my heart and improve.

I chose the latter, and my college experience completely transformed from that moment forward. Nothing felt foreign; I began to feel as if I belonged and quite honestly, I started to feel blessed and worthy of all that I brought to the university. That feeling alone was music to my ears. The earlier you can do this, the better off you will be.

Ask Questions: *Select your major and courses to fit your music.*

My approach to selecting classes was much different entering that second summer. I listened to my heart, and I selected a course that was relevant to me. I heard the music.

That summer I took two courses. Intro to Computer Science was my first selection because I had

Find Your Music

to take it, and I decided it was best to take it during the summer. It was an unfamiliar topic, so I wanted to take the course when I had only one other class to concentrate on, when about three-quarters of the students had left campus and when I didn't have to travel for games.

For my second class, I did something I had never done before. I read through the entire course catalog, searching for a course that spoke to me. When I read the course description of Religions of African Diaspora, I knew that what seemed foreign would be explained, and it was.

I had begun dating my girlfriend (now my wife) about six months before the summer semester. She was (and still is) a wonderful person, and during our early days, she provided a spark of wonder for me at a time when I needed it the most. Early on, I learned that her mother practiced very traditional religious and spiritual concepts—ancient practices that influenced many religions such as Santeria and Candomblé, along with many others. At first, I thought it was weird, only because I didn't understand it, but I wanted to learn more.

I remember picking up my books for the Religions of African Diaspora course. I sat on the floor of Georgetown's bookstore and familiarized myself with each text, and I remember the feeling of wanting to know more. I couldn't wait to see how the professor would address such a topic. I had never been so excited about a course before.

I listened to the music.

I enjoyed the experience of showing up to class

eager to learn about a new subject, prepared and confident that I indeed was ready to contribute; the feeling changed my approach to academics. I immersed myself in subjects that spoke to me, classes that piqued my interest and motivated me to focus on the subject.

Before I fell in love with basketball, writing had been my first love. I would plunge myself into fictional mystery books such as *Goosebumps* and then write my own version of the story. I'd write my mom poems, usually expressing how much I loved her and how much she meant to me. I was no William Shakespeare, but writing allowed me to convey my thoughts and emotions in a completely different format. I can remember searching through the dictionary for words that rhymed and creating different stylistic ways of writing certain words to convey my tones more appropriately.

It was with this same love that I approached my course selection.

When I arrived at Georgetown, not many people could understand the way I spoke, due to my accent. I was never shy about speaking, but eventually I simply chose not to. The fall of my junior year, I decided to take Intro to Public Speaking because I knew it would challenge me. I wanted to become a better public speaker and a more efficient communicator, and this course proved that I could indeed stand shoulder to shoulder with some of the top students at Georgetown.

Becoming a better communicator also accelerated my leadership capabilities on the basketball court and with my teammates. I engaged with my teammates more often and doing so translated to me being a go-to person in the locker room or when a player had a personal issue outside of the gym. My teammates leaned on me, which was a huge turning point in my basketball career.

I approached selecting my classes as an opportunity to pull from the interests of my past, invest in my future and challenge myself academically. The fall of my junior year, I made the Dean's List. It wouldn't be the last time, either. I was just getting started.

Use Your Resources: *Talk to academic advisers.*

Your academic tune is inside you, and everyone's is different. College campuses are resource-rich, so use the resources available to you to find your academic music. Most importantly, use what you know about yourself—your interests and what drives you.

You are responsible for your academic career, but having an academic adviser is awesome. Your coach can't serve for you during a tennis match, but they can guide you to improve your serve. Academic advisers can assist you in achieving your academic goals through illuminating university resources, refining your short- and long-range academic interests and highlighting degree requirements to support your course selection and more. As with any resource, it is all about how you use it.

My first couple of years in college, I met with academic advisers, but most of my time was spent listening and answering their questions. In attempts to get me to open up, they'd ask questions that I had never even thought of, so naturally my initial answers were not very expressive. Don't make this mistake!

Entering college, you may not know your major, but you know your music—understand what academic subjects grab hold of your attention, are aligned with your life and drive you to want to know more. When you know these points, it allows an adviser to do their job more effectively, and it allows you to truly benefit from the resources provided to you.

Build Relationships: *Use those office hours.*

Life is all about building relationships. Whether it's with your coach, classmates, professors, teammates or someone who works in the facilities department on campus, relationships rarely end. For relationships to begin, it takes effort and nurturing for them to flourish.

After practice, we'd always place our sweaty clothes in a mesh bag and drop them off at what was then referred to as *the cage*. The next day, our mesh bags would be in our lockers, fully cleaned and ready for the process to start again. This was new to me, because in high school, we had had to wash our own practice gear every night (and those who didn't could be detected by the nose from a mile away).

At least three to four days a week, I'd see the cage manager, and we'd just talk. I learned about his life, and I felt comfortable enough to tell him about mine. He was a middle-aged Hispanic man. He'd tell me about his children, their vacations or even what he'd had for lunch. I'd talk about Memphis, how I missed my family or even how tough practice was that day. We talked about whatever we wanted.

Over time, a true relationship was formed.

The same principle applies to professors. They're highly accomplished in their field of study and they know a lot, but at the end of the day, they are people just like you and me. Come early to class, stay after class and, especially, take advantage of their office hours. They have deadlines to meet, children at home, vacation plans, as well as messy areas of their lives. They are human.

Getting to know your professors on a personal level will not only benefit you while in college but I can guarantee you those relationships will continue to flourish after you leave the university.

The first time my wife and I returned to campus as parents was a special experience. We'd just returned from two years in Mumbai, India, and wanted to take our two little girls to where we met. We walked into McDonough Arena, Georgetown's on-campus practice gym, and the sight of my daughters running freely across the gym floor made me smile. I knew how much time I had spent within these walls, and not all of it had been pleasant, but seeing their excitement made it all worth it.

After running around the gym for a few minutes, we headed toward the cage, and there I heard a familiar voice: "Omari, my friend, is that you?"

He had aged a bit, and so had I, but we still enjoyed our friendly conversation as we always had.

To introduce him to my two children and stand before him as a married man along with my college sweetheart really hit home the importance of relationship-building. There's no substitute for accumulating that kind of time together. We enjoyed the moment, and catching up with him was the most memorable part of the day.

> *"I speak to everyone in the same way, whether he is the garbage man or the president of the university."* **—Albert Einstein**

Never forget to take the time out to engage with your professors, administrators or campus staff—the people who shape your college experience. If you do, you will never forget them, and they will never forget you. Build a rapport, and establish a relationship built on trust. To do this, just be yourself. We are all imperfect beings.

Try Something New: *See the importance of branching out.*

You are a member of a team; the sport itself brings everyone together, and it is a passion your entire team and coaches share. But everyone is different in their own way and has their own talents. I've had teammates who were really good dancers; one, I remember, was an amazing artist—he could draw whatever he envisioned. Another knew everything about farmland, fishing and almost anything having to do with the outdoors. I had teammates who were plugged into politics, economics, medicine, finance,

Find Your Music

law and more. Each and every one of these talents has an academic component.

Don't be afraid to try something new. You're still young, and you may still be finding your music. At Georgetown, the legendary trainer Lori Michaels loved country music. I had rejected it early in my life, when my uncle Darrell and I would drive around in his car during the summers. He'd all of a sudden turn the radio to a country and western station and say, "Omari, just listen to the words. Country music tells a story."

At sixteen years of age, I couldn't do it! But during my freshman year, after a full day of classes and a grueling practice which had lasted for four hours, I'd lie on a flat table in the training room with Ms. Michaels, and she'd turn on some country music. Instead of rejecting it like a stubborn teenager, I'd listen. Honestly, I didn't have much choice—I was so fatigued I almost felt like I was being held captive.

"Omari, are you listening?" Ms. Michaels would yell while giving me an electro-massage treatment on my sprained ankle. I guess she could sense when my mind was wandering. "This story is about a young love, and if you listen, you'll see where the story goes..."

I'd straighten up, follow the story and focus my mind on the lyrics, the music and the direction of the song. It relaxed me. I began to infuse country music into my rotation when I'd listen to music on my headset on the bus riding to games. Then, during warm-up time, I focused my energy on whatever played on the loudspeaker throughout the arena and enjoyed the moment.

The key to finding your music is focus—focus on your own interests and on areas that may seem unfamiliar to you now but are somehow connected to your natural abilities. Talent doesn't just magically appear: it's woven into your fabric. To identify your many talents, don't be afraid to challenge yourself and push the envelope a little. Find your music, listen to its tune and put your music to motion.

FOLLOW-UP QUESTIONS

1. What brings you joy? What makes your heart sing? What makes you feel alive?

2. Do you have a favorite academic subject? If so, what is it and why?

3. What are some issues facing your hometown, or the town your college is in? How would you address these issues? Plug into the items listed in the chapter and explore available options to integrate those elements into your life and into your heartbeat.

CHAPTER 6

Coaches Blaze the Trail

Throughout my life and career, I've been blessed with the opportunity to work alongside and learn directly from people who have taught me a great deal—especially how to lead and manage diverse groups of people in teams and large organizations.

Whenever these opportunities arise, consider them a coaching lesson.

Coaching comes in many forms. Recently, I had the opportunity to visit a nonprofit organization that specialized in providing service dogs and canine-therapy services to veterans. I'd seen service dogs in action in the past, but once I learned more about how they helped many veterans with physical and/mental-health challenges, it changed my perspective. Today, when I see a service animal, I can better appreciate the countless hours, many trainers and confidence invested into their ability to assist in the natural healing of veterans and their families.

I remember seeing my mother raise our family, sacrifice for others and make tough decisions. I've always admired my mother, but I realized much later she was coaching me the entire time. By watching her I learned how to remain poised and positive when encountered with a conflict situation or a rocky moment in life. Every single day, she provided me with an example to make it through any feat or obstacle I encountered. I saw my dad as the world's greatest truck driver, and I still do even though he's retired. By watching him, I learned how to work hard for what you want; he provided me with the greatest example of how to love what you do and work hard at it. He was coaching me too.

I've also learned a lot from those who have shown examples of how not to lead. I've seen leaders at the highest levels fail to demand ethical responsibility from their employees, and that created a trickle-down effect which damaged the entire company culture. I've been on teams where certain players received special treatment and altered expectations; in the end, the coaches just ended up losing the other players. The team's culture changed, we weren't able to recover and the entire season was affected.

PLANTING SEEDS

Coaches have an immense responsibility, and they plant seeds within their players. Coaching is centered on people, process and philosophy. Coaches can establish a culture of learning and lifelong success.

As you already know, when exposed to positive relationships, players and coaches experience greater satisfaction in life, a sense of self-confidence and strong mental health. These important pillars are personal builders for both coaches and athletes. These attributes will spur an athlete's personal growth in a tremendous fashion—regardless of whether they are second-graders or college-level athletes.

I wouldn't be the global citizen I am today or the person I will become tomorrow without the impact of good, bad and great coaches who influenced me, my life and my future.

YOUTH INVESTMENT

While in high school and college, I always loved coaching younger athletes. It was simple: I'd show them what I did, and I'd introduce them to skills which I was told I needed to do to improve—skills that sometimes I didn't actually follow through in doing, but I wanted them to be aware and equipped with the aids to be better—so I shared. I'd always say, "Be better than me: your improvement improves me." I loved my days as a young player and being a youth camp counselor; these were great experiences and I loved them, just as I enjoy being a youth coach today.

My first official experience being a coach came almost eight years after college. I volunteered to be an assistant coach for a Fairfax County, Virginia, high-school basketball team. I was one of four assistants, so I figured it would be a light commitment because I knew basketball. I'd basically lived the sport and wanted to share my knowledge and global travels with the players. I thought this would be easy. I soon learned that I knew how to play basketball, but I didn't know how to manage and coach a basketball team. That was a very different skill set.

Practice would come to an end, and I'd quickly revert to my player mentality and think, *Yes! It's time to go!* But of course, after practice, the coaching job just gets started—it's time to discuss the practice, review offensive and defensive sets, discuss the upcoming schedule and go over details that as a player I had seen as minuscule, such as what time the team would meet, what they would eat after the game, how the weather affected routes to visiting gyms, etc. These points were, of course, critically important. These were the individual sacrifices that one makes to affect a difference in someone else's life—*this* was the life of a coach. I was flabbergasted by the investment but respectful of the role.

This newfound feeling forced me to reflect on my experience as a basketball player. I remembered the coaches who would come pick me up for practice (during rainy days or thunderstorms) or choose to drive me and two teammates for hours in a crowded car to play in a 3-on-3 tournament. They had lives and families and a million and one tasks that required their attention, yet instead they gave so much: they invested. It wasn't glamorous and didn't come with a deluge of tweets and immediate gratification, but every last one of them did it without complaint, and for that I am extremely grateful.

To ALL my coaches: thank you from the bottom of my heart.

A COACH GETS THE JOB DONE—NO EXCUSES

No two athletic programs are alike. The makeup of the teams is different; coaching philosophies vary; resources rarely are the same; players' skill levels differ. Regardless, the role of the coach is paramount to the balance and overall success of the team—even the definition of *success* is determined by the coach. So regardless of the program, the coach's role in leading the team and defining its mission is key.

In such a significant role, there is no room for excuses—a coach gets the job done.

A good coach can change a game. A great coach can change a life. **—John Wooden, former UCLA head basketball coach**

TRANSITIONS

Athletes are usually in a state of transition—we transfer to a new school, our coaches change, we develop mentally and physically, etc. In college particularly, these are major transitions. And it isn't always easy.

It was my freshman year at Georgetown. I was seated in class, and I looked around and thought, *I can see everybody*. In high school we sat in rows. At Georgetown, we sat in circles in many classes. I felt front and center at all times—this was a transition.

I vividly remember sitting in film sessions, unable to remain attentive because in high school I can count on one hand the times we watched film of ourselves or other teams. On those rare occasions when we did sit and watch film, it was fully isolated on our own team's performance. Our coach didn't believe in following or scouting other teams; we focused on our strategy, nothing else. In contrast, college film sessions were long, methodical and essential to our team's execution both in practice and in the game—this was a transition.

Being away from home, traveling to different parts of the country, missing scheduled classes due to student-athlete travel—these are all transitions. Increased academic and athletic expectations—these, too, are transitions.

As a coach, you are expected to lead student-athletes during one of the most transition-laden points in their lives. It's not an easy task. But you know the score when you sign up. And you know the saying: for unto whomsoever much is given, of him shall be much required.

IN ALL YOU DO, BE MINDFUL . . .

I have one core message for coaches, and it stems from my two decades as a player, my travels across the globe as a sports-diplomacy envoy, my five years as a sports-management professor and my five years of high-school and youth basketball coaching: practice mindfulness.

Mindfulness is the practice of purposely focusing your attention on the present moment and accepting it without judgment.

The seasons are short, while strategically recruiting for the seasons to come is a long process. Players are transferring more and more, which presents an even more challenging environment for coaches to build a program, and the transparency of program administration will continue to allow families to make the decisions that work best for them based on results. On top of that, success is expected, even during rebuilding periods.

So the stress is in full force—that I understand.

But don't let the stress of the grueling season and the pressures of delivering impact how you engage with a youth who is searching for the sport that best fits their abilities or with a college athlete who has a dream but no wherewithal to survive if their dream doesn't come to pass.

A steady practice of mindfulness will allow you to view the whole student, their needs and ways in which you can support that player.

As coaches, you have the ability to find another job or make a career change, but these young minds are fully invested in the opportunity to play sports, represent their schools and see their visions become a reality—it is a dream come true, and it can lead to even more. And remember: they only have four years of eligibility, and they've entrusted them to you, their coach.

We live in a busy world, but practicing mindfulness will allow you to be fully aware of all that is happening in the moment and keep you from being overwhelmed by reactions. It creates a sense of awareness that takes each and every member of the team (players, coaches and managers) into consideration.

I remember the day one of my coaches said something I'll never forget: "You are not here to be smart! You're here to play basketball." I remember feeling like my heart had stopped for a moment, and then it began to pound out of my chest like a bass drum. I was crushed. In that moment, and for months after, I was angry, because I knew that I didn't deserve that admonition and that he was wrong. I knew it came from stress or a horrible place. I've never held a grudge, but I've also never been able to forget it. As a coach, that was a moment to take a deep breath, remember the responsibility and not allow emotions, fear and stress to take over.

I have a great deal of respect for the coaching profession and fully understand the bearing you have on the lives of the student-athletes we all care a great deal about.

Much of the coaching life is dictated by quick decisions. If you don't call that time-out at the right time, momentum could be lost and never regained; if you call a recruit back a day late, they could already have been picked up by another school. These decisions have great impact, but the biggest negative impact you can have is to break a student-athlete's spirit, or to create a dark and gloomy experience at your university, high-school or youth program. And it could all happen due to a decision you made while not being fully aware of your responsibility as a coach.

Coaching my daughters' second- and third-grade basketball team was an exciting time for me. It also came with a great deal of responsibility because I understood that I was coaching future community leaders, engineers, CEOs, mothers, members of the armed services, presidents, etc. Those young girls will be the leaders of tomorrow, and I was their youth coach. I wanted to provide them with the best experience possible; therefore, I had to be mindful of each player and deliver to the best of my abilities. It was my responsibility as a coach.

I want them all to become **Athletes for Life**.

Coaching success isn't measured by wins and losses. Once you reach the moment where you truly understand your players, their needs, goals and the transitions they are going through, you are then tapping into the whole player. You have laid the foundation for success. The more a player feels understood, the better they can positively contribute to the team's mission and accomplish individual goals. *That's* winning.

Keep in mind that you are a light and a flame

for some talented future members of the **Athlete for Life** club. I appreciate your service as a coach, I thank you for your service and I again thank all the coaches who invested in my life and that of my teammates.

Continue blazing trails!

FOLLOW-UP QUESTIONS

1. Identify how a coach affected your life, good, bad, ugly or unmemorably. Now figure out how you can pass on those lessons, or change them in order to pass them on to your fellow athletes, classmates, etc., especially younger ones.

2. Coaches, athletes, anyone really: how do you practice true mindfulness in your day/week? Take time to focus on mindfulness and develop the practice. You will thank yourself later.

3. What are the most admirable character traits that you have learned or witnessed through a coach?

CHAPTER 7

The College Cafeteria

After a long practice, I'd had enough. I was tired. I was hungry. My body ached, and all I wanted to do was get some food and go to bed. Then I looked at the clock; it was almost 8:45 p.m. This was after an intense practice; we had just finished a grueling film session.

This feeling was new for me. In high school, we rarely watched film of other teams, maybe two or three times a season. Our practices were never recorded: who'd record them? We were a basketball powerhouse, but we were still a city school; we didn't have the resources of some of the private schools.

As a freshman at Georgetown, I saw film sessions as either good or bad, with almost no in-betweens. Every practice was recorded, so every mistake you made, every possession you decided to take a break on, every time you didn't help your teammate on defense was there to be viewed, reviewed and critiqued by the whole team. The good film sessions were the ones when your name was never mentioned.

My name got mentioned a lot in this film session—as in, "Omari, look at your effort! Is that all you've got?" When I looked at the clock, I thought to myself, *The café will be closed before I can get there; I'm screwed!* I thought back to my high-school years: if you missed your ride, you were screwed; if you missed lunch and hadn't eaten before practice, you were screwed.

As a young freshman . . . I felt screwed.

After a quick shower, I began walking back toward our dorms with one of my teammates. He was a senior and from the DC area, so I'd always lean on him during those moments of frustration—he had seen it all. I complained a bit about how Coach had ridden me during the film session, and he calmly replied, "You're a freshman. That's what he's supposed to do. Don't sweat it." Then I said, "But the café is closed, and I got no food back in my room," and he gave me a blank stare. At that point I knew I needed to become better prepared and stop complaining so much. My not being prepared was no one's fault but my own.

I hadn't been prepared for a practice that long, and now I'd go to bed with an empty stomach because I was much too tired to wait for order-in to arrive or to find food somewhere off campus. I was screwed.

My teammate hastily burst into a laugh. He said, "Calm down, Slim! We got our own chef for nights like this." Our own chef? What was that? I didn't believe him at first, but I walked with him toward our campus cafeteria, then into some random room around the back. And there it was—our own room and chef.

I was stunned, and I felt relieved.

THE CAFETERIA OF RESOURCES—COLLEGE CAMPUSES

The fact is, college campuses are resource-rich. And as a student-athlete, your experience will be different from others'. You will feel privileged, you will feel different, and with that comes great responsibility.

Imagine you've just entered an amazing cafeteria. Everywhere you turn, there are food, treats and beverage stations that are beyond anything you've ever imagined. I'm talking about juicing stations with any fresh fruit—apples, lemons, pineapples, dragon fruit, grapes and more. Vegetables of all kinds—baked potatoes, corn on the cob, peas, cabbage, etc. Fresh fish, shrimp, lobster, crabs and scallops, fresh cuts of meat, sushi and Korean barbecue. You name it, it's there.

In this type of environment, it would be easy to be overwhelmed and move directly to your favorite dishes, load up heavily on the carbohydrates and meats, and add in a few of your beloved sweets. Before you know it, you'd basically be binge eating. That approach might feel good in the moment, but we all know that won't provide your body with the fuel to perform at its best. If you came across a cafeteria like that, discipline and an understanding of what your body needs would be critical to success.

A college campus is kind of like that. With so many resources, options and avenues, you must pace yourself and focus on the success of your future.

Once you set foot on campus, you quickly realize that it isn't like any other environment that you've experienced before. There are classes and even entire departments devoted to subjects you may have never even heard of. Time is of the essence, and as student-athletes we know that time is limited, but you also have to explore what's on the table in front of you.

Universities are resource-rich, and as a graduate-school professor, I've seen the richness of college campuses firsthand.

I remember my first eighteen months as an adjunct professor at Georgetown University's School of Continuing Studies. I felt like I had come full circle. I was amazed at the programs offered, the services provided to students and just how paramount these offerings were to our leadership culture at Georgetown. I'd think, *Wow, I wish these services had been around when I was in school.* Truth is, they were.

RESOURCES—TAKE ADVANTAGE

The resources that are available to you are abundant, and colleges have rapidly adjusted to a new generation of students with a diverse set of needs and applications. For example, entrepreneurship is a driver for many college students today, so universities have set up and encourage student-led organizations on campus to develop sustainable business plans to solve today's problems and generate revenue streams; these allow the business model to effectively be passed along and improved by the next generation of creative minds.

Most resources are not like mandatory classes. No one will draw you a map and pull you in the door, nor should they. The resources are indeed there, and your presence and past experiences will be an added value to any group on campus or any other resource for the student body. You are a student, yet you are also an athlete, an ambassador for your university. Never forget that.

Here are just a few important resources most universities offer, which all student-athletes should be aware of.

Spiritual Life Office

Faith and spirituality always made up a part of my life and still do today. I can remember as a young child going to church on Sundays with my great-grandmother and all my cousins. It was a really big deal. Dressed in our Sunday best, the entire morning, afternoon and much of the evening were dedicated to worship and fellowship with others.

Most universities today have offices dedicated solely to the enhancement, development and thoughtful encouragement of an evolving spiritual journey for their campus community. This resource allows you to connect with those with a similar background or to explore different faiths around the world.

Georgetown is a Jesuit university. I had really never thought about how I would fit in. I didn't know a whole lot about the Catholic faith, but faith in and of itself was interesting to me. I found the university very open-minded to other religions and faith-based practices; they have a religiously diverse student body and course offerings. I found it fascinating to learn about other religions, as well as study more about my own faith and challenge myself to learn more. Most importantly, I was able to ask questions about religions I had not previously known much about, and I had the opportunity to engage directly with others from backgrounds that proved counter to stereotypes which I had heard in the past.

Today you will have the opportunity to engage in, or even create, spiritually focused charitable programs that benefit local and international communities. Some students might take a semester off to go on mission trips overseas; as a student-athlete, this might not be an option you'd consider, but you never know until you're in that situation and give it some thought. The important thing now is to understand it is an option, and to open your eyes, ears and heart to the idea.

Career Services

Remember: college can prepare you for the rest of your life, and a major piece to the puzzle of life's preparation is finding a career that best suits you. Career-service centers provide a variety of resources that vary based on the institution and their investment in this area. But regardless of their scope, you can benefit from the information they provide and the access to information supporting the next step of your life.

I remember attending career fairs during my senior year and having the opportunity to engage with the Georgetown University alumni community. I enjoyed it, partly because it was similar to pure competition—not that different from my sporting experience. Events were filled with students eager to get a leg up on the competition, and I was there to compete as well. Everyone had what is called a *discriminator*—something that set them apart. Some were campus leaders; some were academic high-achievers and some were just well connected. My greatest discriminator was being a student-athlete—I had played basketball for Georgetown University; how many could say that? I had also become a Dean's-List student and was very proud of my academic achievements. Your academic and athletic career helps you to stand out—use it!

While evaluating universities, seek out universities and colleges that tout their career-services programs. Ask questions like: *What type of career services does your institution provide for its current students and alumni?* Regardless of whether you're a first-round draft pick or your athletic career is over before you graduate, the skills to understanding the professional landscape, which companies hire in your degree path, résumé development, public-speaking skills for interviews and more can travel with you throughout life. You can be a professional athlete with a long career and still be retired at thirty-five. That's a lot of life you've still got to live, and you've got to do something besides count money.

Today, I love attending college career fairs. Having the opportunity to engage directly with today's student population is very inspiring to me. I speak to students about my university experience, and I always find joy in hearing how their current experience is going—the challenges they face or the areas they seek to improve—but the one element that always stands out is the students who are taking advantage of the resources available to them. Hearing them convey how they struggled in a particular area and used available resources to improve their skill set is just plain inspiring.

I see college career fairs as an equal benefit for both employers and students. Employers have the opportunity to engage with and recruit the next generation of leaders, and students have the chance to showcase their talents and be proud of the individuals they have worked so hard to become. All these resources and more can be found through career services, and you don't have to be a senior to take advantage.

Social Clubs and Volunteer Opportunities

During the college years, you have a unique opportunity to learn about other facets of life and to use that knowledge to help define yourself. One important way is through engaging in diverse thought and reflection. Sounds daunting, but really, I'm just saying it's a great chance to activate your passions outside of or through sports. Ask yourself: *What issues matter most to me? If I were ruler for a day, what would I change within my local community or internationally? How do I want to serve?*

I first realized that I had a burning passion for youth development, health care and education while in my last months of high school. I was selected to the Memphis Nike All-Metro Team—a group comprising forty of the city's top men and women basketball players. While I wasn't surprised, it was an honor and dream to be selected.

We had a full two-day schedule of seminars, open practices and public appearances, and the finale was a Saturday evening all-star game which was both entertaining and fulfilling to be a part of. Early that Saturday morning, though, we visited St. Jude Children's Research Hospital, and that was the experience I will remember most vividly from that program.

Our entire group was meeting with children and their families, signing autographs and playing with some of the patients. At one point, I felt overwhelmed. I had had enough. I stormed off—I couldn't take it anymore.

St. Jude was founded and established in Memphis

by Danny Thomas in 1962. Danny Thomas was a comedian, actor and director, but most notably he kept a promise he had made as a young, struggling actor to the apostle St. Jude Thaddeus. He made a vow to build a shrine dedicated to the patron saint of hopeless causes, and his kept promise morphed into a global leader in the advancement of cures and prevention for catastrophic pediatric diseases.

I stood in a hospital bathroom in a total rage. My breathing was heavy, my palms were sweating and tears rolled down my face. I was mad.

I had been visiting with a young girl. The rest of the team, coaches and St. Jude staff had moved along, but I wanted to sit with this little girl who had just undergone months of treatment to cure her body of cancer. She was eleven years old, and when I told her that my jersey number was eleven, she really smiled, and we made a connection. We talked and talked. She told me about her love of reading, and how she couldn't wait to be healthy and get back to school. I shared with her my basketball dreams and how much I'd pray for her. "I will never forget you—you've healed me today," I told her.

One of the team coordinators leaned into the room: "Omari, the group is moving on. We have to go."

I gave her a gentle hug; she squeezed me so tight. I left her room and retreated to the bathroom. I was so upset. I was done. I hated that she and many of the other kids and their families had to experience such an unbearable disease. I wanted to change places with her. I wanted to take her place and give her my health.

At Georgetown, I always supported youth causes. Every summer, I was a youth basketball coach on campus, and my favorite times were the holiday Angel Tree Foundation school visits we'd make as a team to pass out books to kids. My visits back home always included countless hours at daycare centers.

That St. Jude Children's Research Hospital experience changed my life. I am forever grateful for it and for the young girl, who I still pray for today.

College campuses all throughout America have student-led organizations that operate under a mission or a belief, or just the idea of fellowship, and have done so for decades. As a student-athlete, you will have so many opportunities to give. Give of your whole self and look for opportunities to do more and you will not regret it. The sky is the limit.

Every university environment is unique, and it's up to you to decide which on-campus engagement activities work best for you and your interests. No one else.

With any club, the important thing is to get a vibe for the cause and those associated with it. You may have heard great things about a group that advocates for youth literacy within urban communities, but at your university the group could be poorly managed or nonactive. If you feel that your values aren't aligned with an organization and its leaders, you can develop your own cause, collaborate with others and create a group that others will support, endorse and continue for years to come.

I've seen it happen.

Mahatma Gandhi said, "The best way to find yourself is to lose yourself in the service of others." Student-athletes have many avenues to serve and lead on campus. It takes work, effort and follow-up to be impactful, but as athletes, we know about those requirements. The experiences you have outside of sports and outside the classroom are some of the most valuable you'll have in college, and you might not get the opportunities to have those experiences anywhere else in life.

The sooner you engage, the better prepared you will be once that time comes. Take the chance and sample everything the college cafeteria has to offer while you can. And while you're at the table, share your story and just be you. The most important point is that you have a seat at the table; therefore, don't waste the opportunity to embrace nourishing resources which will provide benefits well beyond your days as a college student-athlete.

No child should die in the dawn of life.
—Danny Thomas, founder of St. Jude Children's Research Hospital

FOLLOW-UP QUESTIONS

1. Each month of your college career try your best to walk into one new building. Explore the space. As you walk around, ask yourself: What service does this office provide? Who is this person and what do they do? What did you learn that you didn't know?

2. Think about which resources you need the most. In which areas are you seeking resources and advice?

3. What resources are you (and or others) seeking on campus that do not currently exist?

CHAPTER 8

Transcending Struggles

"I can do anything."

I said that to myself after a class in my junior year at Georgetown. At that moment, I had reached a much deeper level of confidence in my abilities, an understanding of my behaviors and, most importantly, the self-assurance to know that I could indeed climb any mountain. But it wasn't always that way.

CONFIDENCE

I was giving a presentation I'd prepared for weeks. I was explaining why our company should invest a quarter-billion dollars to win a major global IT/logistics opportunity. I was only a quarter of the way through making the case when our company president closed his presentation packet, sat back in his chair and said, "I don't want to do this."

I looked around the conference table and was taken aback. I'd met with everyone else there previously, and they were all on board with my proposal one hundred percent. But once the president, a former one-star general, expressed his displeasure, they all jumped ship and abandoned the operation.

The room went from warm, fuzzy and familiar to me being the lone ranger.

As athletes, we can recognize this scene, right? Many of you have friends, maybe even family members, you face on opposing teams, be it during a pickup game, a friendly sports competition that turns competitive or a league game. You are family, friends, neighbors, but in the land of competition, you don't back down!

That conference room was no different than a basketball court, a track or a lacrosse field. I had come prepared to do my job and do it well. Our group president was also there to do the same. He was a former NCAA basketball player at West Point and had served his country with honor.

I knew his position was taken all in the spirit of competition; I didn't hang my head or take anything personally because I understood that.

Through my research, knowledge of the customer and our company capabilities, I felt this was an opportunity passed by. While everyone else slouched in their seats, I left the meeting unfazed and encouraged to continue forward.

Through sports, you can build confidence that will benefit you throughout your life. As a student-athlete, you won't win every game—sure, there are some anomalies: teams which achieve significant success and go undefeated. But the truth is, we all have experienced losing. We know how it feels to prepare, be ready, feel fearless and yet sometimes lose. The measure of your craft can be seen during times of defeat. Do you wallow in defeat, or do you regroup, retool and prepare for the next competition, meeting, etc.? I learned early in my sporting career to never hang my head in a loss.

Here is another example. While I was a cultural envoy for the Department of State, our program, based around international sports exchanges, was suddenly in high demand across the globe. I'd receive a briefing packet of information from an embassy saying they were expecting fifty to seventy-five participants in a remote province not accustomed to American exchange programs. The next day, I would arrive and there would be three hundred or more young people and their parents, coaches, community leaders and others, waiting excitedly to learn and engage through the universal language of sport.

While embassy staff scrambled to address the need, my confidence stepped in. I would think to myself, *I know sports; I understand people who love sports, and I know how to engage each person who came here today.* And we would do just that.

Having confidence doesn't mean you'll always succeed, but it does mean you approach situations knowing your strengths and unafraid to express your viewpoints.

As a college student-athlete, you will be under extreme pressure and often underneath a microscope. You have to perform in front of hundreds or thousands of screaming fans, maybe millions more watching on TV and online, many of whom are praying for you to fail so they can then criticize you, either in support of their team or just to find affirmation. They think your failure is their success.

I learned that the best way to meet pressure, stress and sometimes doubt is with assurance, preparation and confidence in your abilities.

To do all of the above, understanding yourself is key.

UNDERSTANDING

Whenever you are moving toward a goal or seeking a solution to a problem, you must first understand what the real goal or problem is. To do so, I always recommend self-reflection—an opportunity to understand your attitude, where you are in life and how you can best impact your current situation and similar ones in the future.

Self-reflection can be accomplished in more ways than one.

After practice, I would take long walks in the evenings to clear my head. I'd walk the Georgetown campus and find quiet spots just to be by myself to think and reflect. These were my moments of self-reflection, my opportunities to clear my head.

Some people meditate; others go for a run, speak with a trusted adviser or counselor, listen to music—whatever allows them to pause for a moment and look through a wider lens. These moments build your emotional sensors and self-awareness, which allow you to understand how you are feeling and what's causing you to feel that way.

We made it all the way to the NCAA Tournament my freshman year—the Big Dance. It was an exciting period, but I was too mentally detached to enjoy the ride. We won our first game on a buzzer-beater—a pure March Madness upset over the University of Arkansas, led by a soon-to-be NBA great, Joe Johnson. I burst off the bench in joy with the rest of our team, but inside I was a wreck.

We won our next game too and made it to the Sweet Sixteen. But I wanted to be in the game; I wanted to be the part of the March Madness and feel and taste the success. I realize now that I was a contributing member of the team—I had all that—but I considered my efforts a failure because they weren't what I wanted at the time. A little self-reflection would have helped me out a lot.

SELF-ASSURANCE

Assurance is a positive declaration that builds your confidence. You won't get that from many people, so you have to develop assurance on your own. You can play! You wouldn't be where you are if you couldn't. When you commit your best effort, you are the best.

A university seeks excellence in everything it does, and it seeks the talent to achieve that—at all levels. If you were the leader of a rising travel team, you would want to surround your players with the talent, leadership and opportunities to breed success, from the head coach to the assistant coaches, the team managers, even the bus driver. A university operates the same way. And they picked you.

As a student-athlete, you are a key component to the success of your academic institution. You were not recruited because of luck or by chance. You hold qualities that fit organizations positioned to succeed, and you have to understand this before you get to your college campus. (Or, if you are already in college, make the pivot right now, just as I did.) If you are already a student-athlete, just take a look around. Isn't everyone around you great at what they do? Well, you're with them for a reason, and that reason isn't limited to the sport you play.

STRUGGLE AND TRANSCENDENCE

When I reflect on my time in college, I think of the competing forces which dominated some of my most memorable experiences. During my freshman and sophomore years, I had fallen into a dark place—I was trapped in regret, disappointment and deep depression. Everything I had worked so hard to accomplish was right at my fingertips, but it seemed to be falling apart.

I was not happy.

Being far away from home, in a completely

different cultural environment and not flourishing at what meant the most to me led to a feeling of isolation. My mental health was in a state of decline.

In practice, I could run for hours. I would always finish first and never allow my coaches or teammates to see me impacted by fatigue, which to me was a sign of weakness at the time. My body was strong, but mentally I struggled.

Support found me during this time. I spoke on the phone with my mother almost every day. In these conversations, I'd vent and let out my frustrations, my anger and my resentment. I confided in classmates I trusted; we were all going through similar issues, so the conversation helped. I had my long walks and time by myself. I often found myself inside the chapel on our campus, and there I'd sit in silence and pray.

That moment of self-assurance, when I said, "I can do anything," came during a theology course I took my junior year at Georgetown, called Struggle and Transcendence. This course examined how, when and where God shows up in the experience of black Americans, ranging from contemporary times back to when African slaves were first brought to the New World.

When I was a child, the period of slavery was always intriguing to me. We'd visit antebellum plantations when we lived in Brunswick, Georgia, and I remember being frustrated, upset and mad that people were treated in such a way—people who looked like me, like my family, my friends . . . It just wasn't right.

The principles of this course challenged me to look at life through a different lens. I thought, if my ancestors could arrive in America, work from sunup to sundown and endure incomprehensible hardships, discrimination and intimidation—how could I stand here, at the school of my dreams, in the nation's capital, and regret one moment of my life?

I made a choice: it was time to put myself in high gear and focus on my mental health.

It was the spring semester of my junior year. I had just made the Dean's List for the first time, and I was confident in my abilities, and I understood why the events which caused me pain forced me to seek support.

Mental health is important. As an athlete, there are struggles. As a student, there are struggles. When you look at a mountainous landscape, notice that the mountain peaks are apparent and crystal clear. Underneath those peaks, there are valleys. When you are on top of a metaphoric mountain, there is a sigh of relief because you won and were successful at accomplishing your goal. In the athletic realm, that feeling can change and reverse its course in a matter of hours.

I encourage anyone reading this book to seek the support of friends, family and or a mental-health professional who can provide tools and active-learning exercises to help build your mental health. Seeking help doesn't make you weak; it makes you stronger.

Seek ways to clear your mind often and ensure

your mental health is attended to. During these moments, reflect on your current situation. Here are a few questions to start you off:

What are you most proud of?

Where do you want to be?

Are you happy?

What support do you have available to assist in your goals?

What do you care about the most?

The most important thing to remember is that you are talented and gifted, and though you may have times that are difficult, that is the natural course of things. Whether you choose to take time to spend with family and friends, write in a journal or get out into nature, seek help when you need it, and be confident in who you are. That is the key to success.

FOLLOW-UP QUESTIONS

1. In which moments do you feel most confident? Why do you feel so confident?

2. Take five minutes per day and reflect upon the day's actions and interactions, particularly your response to unexpected events. Becoming more in tune with yourself will only lead to greater inner strength—mentally, emotionally and physically. Here are a few questions to spark self-reflection:

> *What was the most significant thing I did today?*
>
> *What did I learn this week?*

3. Am I putting enough effort into my role as a student? Am I putting enough effort into my role as an athlete?

CHAPTER 9

Parents, Thank You

Parents, I wrote this chapter especially for you. If you are a student-athlete, you can skip it.

Now that we have the children out of the room, let's be honest: your child is the best in the world... because they belong to you. And because they are so talented, ambitious and driven to be better than the rest... Well, let's face it: they're still reading this chapter, even though I sent them away. Why is that? Because they want to be the best at what they love.

So let's have an open conversation.

Some of you parents are former (or current) athletes, like me. The understanding of sports, the rules of engagement and attention to detail isn't anything new: you get it. Some parents and/or mentors are new to athletics in general, though:

your child's situation presents a new experience for everyone involved. You might feel at times a bit out of your element because, frankly, you just don't get it. How could you?

But even if you bring a lot of prior knowledge to the sport your child is submerged in, the likelihood that they will have the same athletic journey you did is . . . not impossible, but pretty remote. And even if they do have a similar pathway, the times and the game have changed; therefore the journey itself will be altered.

The important mechanism is that you embrace this gray area and try not to let it make YOU gray through stress and worry. Your child will be just fine. The fact that you have taken your time to read this book means you are invested and understand the positive benefits of athletics. You care about what kind of a parent you are to your student-athlete, and that's the most important thing.

ACADEMICS: FIRST THINGS FIRST

"You coming to practice today, Omari?" a teammate asked me. I responded in the negative, with an expression of disappointment and annoyance. This happened a lot my sophomore year in high school. I missed more than ten games during the middle and end of the season and countless practices, as my mom and stepdad pulled me off the team. Why would they do that? Because of my poor classroom performance. According to the school's academic standards, I was eligible to play, but I was not eligible based on my mother's expectations.

I remember these as some of the darkest and most frustrating days of my high-school experience, and there was no way to really explain to anyone else why I couldn't play. Everyone just thought *Omari has some really strict parents*, and they were right. My mom would not budge when it came to my academics. While I hated it at the time, my mom set the bar. I veered off course many times, yet her standards always remained. That bar finally led me back to a place where I was confident in my academic abilities and propelled me to becoming a Dean's List student and a balanced student-athlete at Georgetown University.

From the moment your child becomes a student-athlete, there will be a myriad of distractions—intense practice schedules, video games, cell phones, travel games, etc. The important thing is setting that bar early—making sure your child fully understands that academics come first and there are no questions about it.

We parents know our children, and those of us with multiple children also understand that no two offspring are the same. So while my mother's firmness worked for me, pulling your child off the team may not work for yours or in every situation. But I encourage you to have very candid conversations with your child that align your academic standards with their academic abilities. Student-athletes are full of ambition and potential beyond our imagination. While some will be self-motivated, others might need constant reminders or, as I needed, an enforcer.

Use these lessons to set the bar:

Listen

Once your child comprehends that you are fully vested in understanding and supporting their athletic journey (which isn't always pretty), this opens the opportunity for them to fully understand you. Being a parent to a student-athlete comes with challenges, and expressing these to your child isn't always a bad idea. For this to happen, though, there must be an open dialogue. Everyone needs to be able to listen, communicate directly and convey expectations.

I always encourage parents to be active listeners by focusing directly on what their child is expressing and asking questions to further understand their viewpoint. My mother was a master of this while I went through some rough times at Georgetown. We'd talk, and I'd vent my frustrations, sometimes going on and on. Most of the time, she would just listen and allow me to fully express myself. Now, as a parent myself, I understand that wasn't always easy to do. But it helped me significantly. Thanks, Mama!

Active listening improves relationships and allows for progressive dialogue. Once the culture of active listening is embraced, this allows you to set clear expectations and always remind your child whenever they are veering away from those set and established expectations, goals and mission priorities.

Recap

Once your expectations have been clearly conveyed, recap your discussion, and be sure everyone is on the same page. During time-outs, whether it's the first game of the season or the last game with a championship on the line, great coaches ensure everyone understands the instructions and expect the team to execute. If an athlete runs away from the huddle unclear or confused, there is a strong possibility that errors will occur.

I personally am a fan of writing things down on paper: you see it and can touch it. While this may not be the preferred style for most, try something that fits your style, but be sure it is clearly understood.

Implement

There is no excuse for not placing importance on academics. This must be clear. If your student-athlete wants to play in every game, attend practices and have fellowship with teammates, they have to show the same application to their academic effort, being attentive and engaged in class, showing consideration to classmates and delivering to the best of their abilities. Academics will be a major component to becoming a better teammate and also a better **Athlete for Life**; for them to achieve this, you as the parent, must set these standards, and the sooner the better. If you set parameters without ensuring their implementation, that's almost worse than setting none at all.

A coach tells the team to be at practice no later

than 6:15 p.m. or they will not play in Friday's game. If a player comes waltzing in at 6:23 p.m. without a justifiable reason and plays in the game Friday, think of the message it sends to players who do follow the rules—and the message it sends to the player who disregards the rules.

Children usually love, admire and respect their parents. At the end of the day, student-athletes want to see their parents proud of them, and just as they're continuing to read this chapter, they will not follow directions at times—no one is perfect. But in the end, they come through when it really counts.

HANDLING THE STRESS

From the start, my journey was a stress-filled one for my parents.

I started on my high-school varsity basketball team as a freshman. I hadn't played organized basketball as long as most of the other players, so everything was new to me, and I was a bit like a young, goofy baby deer. I had natural athletic ability, but was still learning the game, and my mother was protective of my time and attention to the sport. (Besides, I was the youngest, so I was her baby.)

I vividly remember a home game midway through the season. During the second half, I back-pedaled down the court, and just as I approached half-court, I was met with a screen from the opposing team's center that also included a sharp elbow to the center of my throat. It caught me completely off guard, and I fell hard to the floor. It took a moment for me to regain my vision as the wind had been completely knocked out of me.

As I lay still on the floor surrounded by my teammates, trying to regain my sight and breath, I looked up and thought, *Wow, that's my mom's underwear.* Sadly, I wasn't hallucinating. I shook my head to snap out of it and saw my mom charging from her usual seat and throwing her leg over a four-and-a-half-foot median, with someone from below helping her scale what seemed like the Great Wall of China. She greeted me on the court just as I stood up, and I assured her that I was just fine.

I was kind of embarrassed, but I also saw the stress and worry in her eyes.

As a parent, I totally understand how protective of our children we can be; we care and express our concern in various ways.

My senior year in high school, I could be labeled as *the man*. I was good and exciting to watch, but I had my flaws like everyone else—and with a target on my back, many opposing teams came directly after me. I remember being elbowed in the face once, maybe intentionally, but it didn't matter. I shook it off and headed back down the court. Contact happened a lot, but this time, I tasted something running down my face and into my mouth as I approached the half-court line—it was blood, and lots of it. I put my hand over the wound to my left eye, and when I looked at my blood-drenched hand, I fell dramatically to the floor.

Just like my freshman year, I was surrounded by my teammates and my coach yelling, "Get up off the

Parents, Thank You

floor," because he saw falling and lying on the floor as a sign of weakness. I rose to my feet and looked over to my dad. He hadn't moved one bit. He had the same look of stern calmness on his face that he had every game.

That night, my dad took me to the emergency room, where I received eleven stitches over my eye. I thought I looked cool, like a boxer. As we sat in the emergency room with a blood-stained bandage over my eye, I remember looking at my dad as he sat next to me, still in his work clothes, which had a familiar stench from a long, hard day's work as one of Memphis's finest truck drivers. He turned to me and said, "Son, you have got to get back on defense faster."

He handled it his way; my mom handled it hers. But they both did their best. And you know what? He may have been playing it cool, but I saw the stress in his eyes too.

All parents have to find their place in the life of a student-athlete. You play the role that fits best for you and your child. As parents, we know that some children need a little more encouragement than others, and sometimes encouragement comes in the form of criticism, yelling and demanding even more. Sometimes it can mean letting our child fight through their pain, rise to their feet and push through it. Either way, it comes with stress and fatigue, and it's often a thankless job.

Your child might not thank you all the time, or maybe ever, but they really do appreciate all that you do. Even if they don't recognize it now, they will. The money required to support student-athlete's needs, and the time and travel required to be at games, practice and tournaments (local and out of state) isn't easy to come by.

Everyone's circumstances are different. Some parents can't be as present or as involved in athletic activities, and I'm sure that can be just as difficult. Most parents want to be there, engaged and cheering, but life doesn't always present that option.

I can remember missing my mom at my games when I moved back home to Memphis to live with my dad. I also missed my dad when I stayed in Georgia with my mom. At Georgetown, I missed them both at games, but I always knew what they expected of me, and the presence of their values never left me.

Whichever situation you're in, my advice is the same as it is to student-athletes: do the best you can and be yourself. And I have the same advice for you that I just gave your child: if you're at this level, you must be doing something right. Congratulations, parents, and best wishes!

FOLLOW-UP QUESTIONS

1. The fact that you have taken your time to read this chapter (or entire book) means you are invested in your child's academic and athletic development; you care a lot, and that is key.

2. If you consider yourself an **Athlete for Life**, what lesson from your experience is most important to share with your child?

3. If you never played a sport, what was something you did that you worked hard at and pushed yourself? What did that teach you? Share the lesson with your child that playing a sport isn't the only thing that makes you an **Athlete for Life**.

CONCLUSION

When a game ends, a new one always begins. It is with this simplicity that I view this manual's conclusion. As I stated during the introduction, I wrote this manual to outline the importance of connecting with the athlete in all of us and to document actionable steps for current and future student-athletes to implement. I opened up my own diaries, read the words I had written and transported myself back to my middle school days, high school years and college journey. It was in those moments that I asked myself, "What type of book would inspire me to change course and do better right now?"

The **Athlete for Life** initiative was founded on this reflection and has the power to impact generations of student-athletes for years to come.

As I think back on my journey to this point of penning my very first book, it was a challenging process! Why? Because I have never written a book before. There were many questions along the way: How do I start? Should I just write and structure the book later, or do I begin with organization, etc.? At certain crossroads, I found it perplexing to commit myself to writing a book because I couldn't decide on what type of book I wanted to write. Now, as I write this final chapter, this finished product is a testament to the importance of dedicating oneself to a project or idea that will benefit others. That was my number-one goal from the beginning, and through every roadblock or question, I never stopped.

Then something magical happened.

I continued to think of the countless number of former student-athletes that might not be connecting the dots from their academic and athletic experiences to their current lives. I met with thousands of former athletes and current student-athletes, and from these discussions, I saw a gap that needed to be filled. As I became more entrenched in the current state of youth sports, I wanted to share my story and lessons learned to provide a bonding agent for athletes traveling along the same road I had once traveled.

This has been my inspiration and the driver that has led me to this final chapter of a book that I am extremely proud of.

YOUR SPORTS JOURNEY: HOW IS IT DEFINED?

The treasurable experience of sports can drive one beyond measure. A sports journey isn't determined by how many points your child averages in their third-grade basketball league or how many hits you make in youth baseball, nor is it even about your regional ranking in high school. A sports journey isn't determined by whether you make your high-school team or are offered an athletic scholarship after graduation. And I can assure you that your sports journey isn't measured by your ability to make it to the professional ranks.

A journey is simply a passage from one point to the next, and your sports journey is defined by you.

Years after graduating from Georgetown, there was a period in my life when I wanted to move past being defined or labeled as an athlete or a former NCAA basketball player. I wanted nothing to do with that "former" part of my life. Whenever I met someone new who didn't know of my past, I never talked about my sports experiences; if they somehow found out, I'd downplay the experience. One day my wife, who always boasts about my student-athlete career and my time as a sports envoy, told me very directly, "What you experienced as an athlete was amazing. You should be proud and never downplay an experience many could only dream of." At that very moment, I began a revamped journey, which later morphed into me becoming an **Athlete for Life**.

GIANTS

Whether you are a student-athlete, a parent to a student-athlete, or a coach to student-athletes, we are all blessed to be in such a position. While the road isn't easy, we are undeniably in possession of a talent that affords us the ability to be not only stellar students and athletes but also leaders and examples of mental strength, life balance and wisdom. I will never forget when I saw this example for the first time in my life.

I had just moved back home to Memphis, Tennessee, the summer before my junior year in high school, and there was no question about which school I'd attend. My parents met at and graduated (along with many other family members) from Hamilton High School, and so would I.

That summer I worked out with my Hamilton High teammates and had the opportunity to get to know the entire team. One of my teammates, Michael Moody, always stood out. That summer he was a rising senior and was the backup point guard for our team, and I loosely use the term backup because our starting point guard, Antonio Rambo, was the toughest competitor I've ever seen to this day; therefore, a backup wasn't necessary. Moody's playing time on the court was sporadic, but his role on our team was colossal as he was the glue, the balance and the leader who always held our team together.

Moody set the bar high. His approach to school was serious and determined. While some joked around during study hall, I'd look at Moody, and without saying a word, it was obvious that he was focused and wasn't for one second joking around during our window of study before practice. He never cared much about fashion trends or what was considered cool at the time; he was intent on accomplishing his long-term goals. Moody was a model student-athlete and an inspiring teammate on and off the court, and that is why I could think of no one else more fitting to dedicate this book to. He was a living example of a true model student-athlete. I admired his poise, his focus and the vision he maintained for his future—an unlimited future, no matter the barrier; he'd either break through it or find a way around it.

I walked through the front doors of Hamilton High School one day during my senior year, and there on the loudspeakers, I was shockingly greeted with words I will never forget. My teammate, Michael Moody, had died in a car accident. He was a freshman in college and had become what he always wanted to be, a Morehouse man. Moody shared the same birthday as Martin Luther King Jr., so when he was accepted into Morehouse College (also MLK's alma mater), he knew it was a blessing.

Here is an excerpt from a scholarship essay of his:

> Acknowledging that God is the reason for my being, determination, hard work, and a sound education are the forces that drive me personally, professionally, and academically. Of the three, I consider education to be the greatest. In conjunction with fire, water, earth, wind, and love, I hold education to be the sixth element to man's existence. The more I excel academically,

Conclusion

the more I realize how academics helped me to reach my full potential and tap into who I truly am. The philosophy of determination, hard work, and a good education was instilled in me at a young age. Recalling as far back as swimming classes at the YMCA for four-year-olds, I never once heard my mother complain about her role as a single parent. Instead, what she taught me was despite present conditions I could achieve anything I desired. She taught me to make the best of life and build in the positive in each situation. When faced with the reality of bearing the full cost of my college tuition, my mother responded by reminding me there was no substitute for a good education regardless of the cost. She wanted me to understand there were some things in life that could not be measured in terms of money but in terms of the quality they provided in enhancing one's life.

When I reflect on my academic achievements, I can appreciate my third grade teacher for challenging me to produce more than mediocre work. Her goal for her students was to excel above and beyond their everyday environment of standard living. As a result of my school, church, and community involvement, it was easy for me to consciously excel in high school. I have always accepted the fact that "I am my Brother's Keeper." My desire has always been to create a positive impact on the lives of my brothers, sisters, and community.

I was determined to be counted among the number with Martin Luther King Jr., Benjamin Mayes, Thurgood Marshall, and the list of other brilliant black men. I worked diligently to be better than good academically and socially. Attending Morehouse College has heightened my determination and drive to become a successful entrepreneur.

It is key to remember the **Athlete for Life** journey never ends; it is a continuum throughout life, and we must share our experiences with those that come behind us, those who look up to us and be sure to pave a brighter path for our globe's future athletes.

"If I have seen further than others, it is because I have stood on the shoulders of giants." While this famous quote is attributed to Sir Isaac Newton because he used the expression in a letter he wrote in 1676, he was actually paraphrasing. The full simile was said by Bernard of Chartres, a 12th century French philosopher:

> We [Moderns] are like dwarves perched on the shoulders of giants [the Ancients], and thus we are able to see more and farther than the latter. And this not at all because of the acuteness of our sight or

the stature of body, but because we are carried aloft and elevated by the magnitude of the giants.

Becoming an **Athlete for Life** transforms you into a giant. Through your example, you will provide others with the mental and physical strength, stamina, determination, and fortitude to accomplish mission objectives, build families and communities, and push through the difficult moments in life. And most importantly, your example will provide a plateau for the future generations to stand afoot and be bolder, more confident and assured that their athletic passions and abilities are never dated.

SURPRISE OF MY LIFE

"How would you like to come play for our professional club team? We'll pay you handsomely and provide you housing, a car and trips to see your family twice during the season." I heard these words from a friendly (and awestruck by my athleticism) Egyptian sports manager. As a U.S. Cultural Envoy for the U.S. Department of State only two months removed from college graduation, those words were music to my ears. "Does this sound like something you'd be interested in?" I thought to myself, *This is a dream come true. I will officially be a professional basketball player, getting paid for playing a game that I have loved for so long.* I had a major decision to make.

The U.S. Embassy in Cairo, was leading our

cultural exchange activities throughout Egypt, and I had the honor of meeting the Egyptian National Basketball team's coaches and players. After a gracious introduction, I sat and watched the team run through drills and a warm-up session. All I could think was, *Wow, these guys are representing their entire country, and they are darn good!*

A translator from the U.S. Embassy staff pulled me aside and said, "They would like you, the American basketball player, to teach them some U.S. drills to improve their basketball skills." I explained to her that from what I had witnessed, playing together would allow us to learn from each other and gain the most out of this opportunity. That was just what we did.

The day before this event, I made my way to a restaurant by the Nile River. I sat in awe, just taking in the scene. I had admired this body of water all my life, and the river that had fundamentally shaped Egypt's amazing history was right before my eyes. I thought of the river's history, its power and all those who had explored different journeys above and beneath the surface. This moment shined a light on just how far my very own sports journey had taken me.

Playing in an exhibition game with the Egyptian National Basketball team was a thrill and my first time playing so extensively with true professionals. These were mostly adult men who had being playing for a very long time; some had even played in competitive European leagues. I held my own and played very well. The offer to play for the Egyptian

Conclusion

Basketball League was deeply meaningful to me as I knew many roads to the NBA started by playing on the international circuit.

What I had dreamed about my entire life was well within my reach—I could become a professional basketball player.

I self-assuredly declined the offer within minutes during our conversation. I needed no time to think or ponder the possibilities. Why? Because I was enjoying the exploration of other parts of the deep sea of sports. I was traveling the globe to connect people of different cultures using sports as the vehicle to understand each other as a human race. I'd made it! I loved the work I was accomplishing at the Department of State, and I wanted to take all that I'd learned through sports and apply it to areas of international diplomacy and beyond. (This particular journey might just be my next book. It was unbelievable!)

Looking back, I know that moment was major, but what was more momentous and shocking was that I made that decision so quickly. As athletes, we are often placed in high-pressure situations that require rapid decisions to be made. Sometimes it's our natural instinct since the countless hours of practice improve our instincts, training us to rapidly adapt and allow for speedy reactions. This was one of those moments for me. It felt like the last seconds of a championship game—no time-outs, and the ball was in my hands. When you know it, you know it—take the shot!

I've never regretted that decision.

EVOLVE

When I arrived at the historic front gates of Georgetown University, I never imagined that I would someday return as a professor and a member of the Board of Governors and would contribute to numerous advisory boards, committees and bodies that determine the future of our university. This wasn't my dream that day I arrived but neither was it far beyond the realm of what I could achieve once I put my mind to something.

As individuals, we evolve. Teams evolve, families evolve and dreams evolve.

Today, as student-athletes (or as parents to student-athletes), you are almost birthed into a competitive environment. Youth programs are becoming more structured in ways that mimic high school or college-level play, and professionalized sports skills training begins earlier and earlier it seems. I say this not to be negative but to highlight the fact that there are many changes transpiring within the sports field today; change in many cases can be positive, but any change without the awareness that change is happening can leave someone unprepared and vulnerable to that particular shifting landscape.

That is why I say, be yourself; be proud of who you are and where you are because you are evolving with every second. I began college unprepared, and my priorities were completely off, but that had no impact on how my college career evolved and the legacy I was able to establish once I made the decision to be a complete student-athlete. As an **Athlete**

Conclusion

for Life, you will be faced with challenges, opportunities, threats and much more. As leaders, stand firm at the sight of challenges, and always remember you are equipped to overcome adversity. To do so, understand your resources, utilize those resources and remember that your journey is evolving and never ends. You are an **Athlete for Life**!

"Remember life isn't always what we planned, but sometimes what WE planned and want isn't always what's planned for us!" **—Mom Rey, my mother-in-law**

ACKNOWLEDGMENTS

I want to thank my family as they remain my greatest strength. Had it not been for them, this book would not be possible. I thank them for all that they have invested in me throughout the years. The ironclad foundation that my ancestors so solidly paved for my family fuels me with energy and such a profound optimism for the future. Mama, Daddy, Moon and Akilah—you all have been with me since day one; I heard your voices before I took my first breath, and you are with me forever and always. I love you.

To Mr. Harris, Grandpa Rey and Nana—I love you and I am forever grateful to have you as parents and a part of my family. I've learned countless lessons from you all and continue to do so today.

And to Mable Rey, my mother-in-law, I feel your presence from above. In what seemed like a short period of time we bonded beyond measure and I miss you dearly. I know you are soaring with the angels and I feel your wings wrapped around us all. I love you.

As a parent to very active children, I thank God for them. Presley, Kinley, Hailey and Harley (and our chubby pug Vixen), you keep me energized and motivated. I love you dearly. Being your Dad means the world to me and just witnessing your growth over the years and your own individual personalities continuing to flourish is a dream come true. Seeing you enjoy school and the excitement in which you approach learning is a blessing. You make me so proud. Coaching your youth basketball team has added so much value to my life, and I want to say thank you so much for your patience and understanding. I know being the coach's kid isn't always easy, but you all amaze me with your ability to lead, fall and jump back up, and I thank you for always being honest with me. You make me a better man, daddy and coach! Thank you, girls. I love you.

To Rick Massimo: From the start, I valued your body of work and knew that we could create something special because you were original, and I felt you never second-guessed taking on any project I tossed your way. I appreciate your adoration and respect for art and culture, and it is through that lens that I connected with you the moment we were introduced. Over the years, you have offered so much literary advice and have pushed me to be a more expressive writer. In the beginning, when I tried to focus less on my journey, you encouraged me to dig deeper and tell more.

To Carole Sargent: You introduced me to Rick Massimo and for that, I thank you. You also inspired me to write, think outside the box and encouraged me to reinvent the narrative. Our conversations were really inspiring, and I thank you for being you and your honesty throughout the process.

To all my teammates: Throughout the years, we have had some fun times. We have experienced wins and losses, we have fought among ourselves, we have accomplished the impossible when everyone counted us out, we have mourned the loss of our very own, we have held each other's children and we continue to support each other today. For all of those reasons and many more, I thank God for allowing me the opportunity to participate in team sports. We all learned a great deal together, and when I look back on my experiences today, we were learning so many lessons about courage, integrity, grit, grind, passion and more. And most of the time, I was completely oblivious to the fact that these lessons were being ingrained into our fabric. I thank you all for supporting this book, and thanks for being my teammates—much love!

To my teachers and coaches: you all have left footprints on my life in ways you probably wouldn't even believe. Many of you were patient with me, and some of you gave me the nudge I needed to get in gear. I could write an entire book on just how much you pushed me and inspired me, and you remain a major reason why I put so much effort into this book; your belief in me activated me on many levels. Throughout my career, I've been blessed to have hundreds of teachers and coaches: teachers, teacher's assistants, principals, counselors, head coaches, assistant coaches, camp coaches, AAU coaches, etc. There is no way I could name you all, so I want to leave only a few quotes that I wrote down over the years, and you know who you are. Thank you!

> *"I see the potential in you, and now you must see the potential in yourself."*

> *"Omari, I am offering you a full scholarship— room, board, books, tuition and the opportunity to change your life forever."*

> *"As a coach and teacher, you just want your players to stay out of trouble and grow up to be real men and women, family leaders and responsible tax-paying citizens. I am proud of the man, father and husband that you have become."*

> *"You breathe life into me. I know your voice and your story will instill hope and action into millions someday."*

During the very beginning stages of writing a book, I sat down with a talented writer and editor with whom I had been working on a few projects. We discussed the idea of why I wanted to write and then it took me more than a year (or two) to settle on the book I felt would be most beneficial. While we didn't work together on the book, that first conversation was important and I thank you for agreeing to step in at the very end to support some finishing touches. That meant a lot—thank you, Stefanie Manns.

To my wife, Marquex: You have witnessed my student-athlete transition up close and personal since day one. Your impact on this book has been equal to mine and for that I am truly grateful. I thank God for aligning the stars and the rest is history. You read the first draft, coached me through writer's block, kept me on schedule and so much more. I love that you remain the leader of academic excellence for our family and you've led the charge within our local educational community—an imprint that will last for generations to come. When we started dating in college, you were the finest example of a student I had ever seen. Witnessing firsthand your effortless, yet dedicated work ethic inspired me beyond belief. It changed my approach. From the start, you saw something in me, and I saw something in you; that something has moved mountains in my life and built monuments that will last through eternity. Together we've created a story that I can tell a trillion times and never be bored. I thank you from the bottom of my heart for giving your all to this book project. I am at my best when you are with me. Thank you Love!

To all current and prospective student-athletes, remember this: Being a student-athlete is not easy. There will be stress and moments when you want to quit, and then there are the moments when you find balance and the hard work (and the hard work of so many that helped you get to that point) pays off. It is during those moments that you achieve the balance required to become an **Athlete for Life**. I challenge you to pay it forward and teach another student-athlete the principles. For that, I thank you in advance.

ABOUT THE AUTHOR

OMARI FAULKNER is a trailblazing corporate executive, global strategist, professor, author, diplomacy expert and a Public Affairs Officer in the Navy Reserves. Omari attended Georgetown University, where he was a member of the men's basketball team. While at Georgetown, he received many awards and distinctions for his contributions on the court and in the classroom - a few of his recognitions include Big East All-Academic Team, an NCAA Sweet 16 appearance, and Georgetown Dean's List.

After graduating from Georgetown University, Omari served as an International Goodwill Ambassador for the U.S. Department of State's high-profile sports/cultural diplomacy program, traveling to more than 45 countries as a U.S. Sports Envoy. He served at the State Department in a number of capacities including Financial Management Officer, and Human Resource Officer. His exemplary service in these roles has earned him national recognition and prestigious distinctions around the world.

Mr. Faulkner provides executive thought leadership to numerous organizations and strategic insights within Fortune 500 companies, universities, and non-profit organizations. He has built a federal civilian growth strategy and a multibillion prospective revenue stream for a leading solutions provider to the federal government. Today, as the company's Brand Ambassador, he manages strategic partnerships, veteran and military affairs, inclusion and diversity outreach and workforce development initiatives.

For Mr. Faulkner, success and service are synonymous. In 2014, he founded O Street International, a non-profit organization missioned to support cultural and educational diplomacy programs both domestically and globally. He remains attuned to the landscape of education and is currently an adjunct faculty member at Georgetown University teaching master level courses on Sports Leadership and Management, Global Social Responsibility, etc.

Celebrated for his work and commitment to higher education, philanthropy, and sports leadership, Omari is the recipient of hundreds of awards and recognitions domestically and internationally, including Georgetown University's Excellence in Teaching Award and the U.S. State Department Superior Honor Award. Omari also speaks to audiences around the world on a wide range of topics such as workforce development, student-athlete success, diversity, diplomacy and leadership. Today, he serves on a number of advisory committees and boards, advocating for quality education, service and volunteerism, economic development, veteran affairs and history preservation.

Omari lives with his wife and their amazing four children in Loudoun County Virginia.

Twitter—@omari_faulkner
#AthleteForLife

CPSIA information can be obtained
at www.ICGtesting.com
Printed in the USA
BVHW030548040720
582952BV00002B/417